Wise Wealth

Wise Wealth

Creating It, Managing It, Preserving It

Joachim Schwass
Professor of Family Business, IMD, Switzerland

Håkan Hillerström
Independent Advisor

Holger Kück
Advisor

Colleen Lief
Research Associate, IMD

palgrave
macmillan

MyCopy version of the original edition 2011

First published 2011 by
PALGRAVE MACMILLAN

Palgrave Macmillan in the UK is an imprint of Macmillan Publishers Limited, registered in England, company number 785998, of Houndmills, Basingstoke, Hampshire RG21 6XS.

Palgrave Macmillan in the US is a division of St Martin's Press LLC, 175 Fifth Avenue, New York, NY 10010.

Palgrave Macmillan is the global academic imprint of the above companies and has companies and representatives throughout the world.

Palgrave® and Macmillan® are registered trademarks in the United States, the United Kingdom, Europe and other countries.

DOI 10.1057/9780230295278

A catalogue record for this book is available from the British Library.

A catalog record for this book is available from the Library of Congress.

10 9 8 7 6 5 4 3 2 1
20 19 18 17 16 15 14 13 12 11

Transferred to Digital Printing in 2014

Springer.com/mycopy

To the families of the world struggling to find their own path: If we can help just one family, we will feel gratified and content in the knowledge that we have shared our experiences and expertise for the betterment of families in business.

Contents

List of Tables and Figures

Tables

Figures

Preface

We, the authors of this book, have been fascinated with the evolution of private wealth – entrepreneurship, family businesses, family offices and the entrepreneurship of the next generation. We have experienced and studied many aspects of wealth – creating, managing and preserving it for the long run, for the benefit of as many generational descendants as possible. In recent times, each of us has become deeply concerned with two dimensions: first, the increasing volatility around wealth; and second, the enormous difficulty of keeping wealth together throughout generations.

Never before have there been so many opportunities to create wealth in a relatively short period of time. The emergence of new industries, especially in the areas of finance, technology and real estate, has seen an explosion in the number of millionaires and billionaires. A new generation is growing up, mesmerized by how easy it can be to get rich quickly. Yet members of the senior generation are shaking their heads, as they remember the hard work it took to create wealth from nothing – especially those who experienced wars and other important disruptions. Are we indeed seeing paradigm changes in which the rules of the game are altered forever? Or was the 2008 financial crisis a painful reminder that wealth creation and management are not that easy, after all? What is certain is that volatility has increased, on both the upside and the downside. It is equally certain that some wisdom on how best to deal with this new situation is needed.

We have, individually and jointly, over decades, gained insights into and experience of the way entrepreneurs and families deal with the opportunities and challenges of preserving wealth for the benefit of future generations. We agree that in the long run this is extremely difficult. In fact, wealth destruction over time seems inevitable: Sometimes by the very founder who cannot imagine a business where everything is no longer meticulously controlled by him or her; sometimes by the next generation of siblings who fight for control; sometimes by cousins who cannot agree on a shared vision for their diversity of interests and needs. It is hard enough to keep a family business healthy and growing. It is even more difficult to keep together and functioning well a family office, which structures investments and liquidity for the family. Money is more volatile than businesses.

We have combined our personal, academic and professional experiences and perspectives with the objective of writing a book that:

- Gives broad and deep insights into relevant aspects – especially continuity – of private wealth.
- Uses pragmatic frameworks and proven concepts from advanced family business research.
- Provides new insights into the growing field of family offices.
- Expresses our – sometimes uncompromising – views.

We want not only to shed light on how to understand better the challenges and opportunities throughout the phases of creating, managing and preserving wealth for future generations but we want also to offer guidance, recommendations and judgments on what works best. In order to demonstrate one family's journey through the evolutionary cycle, we will use the story of the Owens family as a "red thread" throughout these pages. The changing Owens family tree can be found in Appendices A and B.

This book is written for entrepreneurs, families in business, families with wealth and all concerned stakeholders and service providers. For simplicity's sake, we have often referred to the protagonists of this story as "he." But we acknowledge the role of women in this evolutionary process, both behind the scenes and on the front lines. The growing number of women entrepreneurs renders them a powerful force in the present and the future. Our focus is on continuity, and we believe that next generation descendants of the wealth creators will draw particular benefits from our insights. Our target group also includes individuals and families who suddenly find themselves in the fortunate position of having some wealth and who wonder about the future.

Creating wealth is difficult. So is managing it effectively. Losing wealth is the easiest part. In our experience, in many cases this can be avoided. But it takes an enlightened approach to attempt to understand future issues and to prepare and plan – for the benefit of the next generations.

Acknowledgments

This book could not have been written without the support of IMD.

Many people deserve the authors' thanks for having contributed – knowingly and unknowingly – to this book. First and foremost, we are indebted to all the families mentioned in this book, and in particular to Richard Owens, for allowing us to use his case as a red thread throughout the chapters. We are also grateful to Michelle Perrinjaquet, Lise Moeller and Megan Price at IMD for their continuous support. Finally, our special thanks go to Lindsay McTeague, IMD Senior Editor, for her patience and tireless support in making this a better book.

About the Authors

Joachim Schwass is Professor of Family Business at IMD business school in Lausanne, Switzerland where he directs the Family Business Center. He has studied at the TU in Berlin and earned his doctorate from the University of Fribourg. He grew up in a family business, has held CEO positions in various companies around the globe, and is an active owner in his own family business. For almost twenty years he has studied and educated leading family businesses around the world. Professor Schwass sits on the board of directors of the Family Business Network International in Lausanne. He is the author of numerous articles and case studies on the subject of family business and entrepreneurship. His book *Wise Growth Strategies in Leading Family Businesses* was published in English, German, Spanish and Chinese.

Håkan Hillerström has been an independent advisor and coach since 2003. He serves families in business by helping them to craft solutions in family governance, strategic and continuity planning, and wealth management. Having previously worked for seven years in the PricewaterhouseCoopers family business practice, he is well placed to offer advice to clients around the world. Mr. Hillerström holds an MBA from IMD and lectures frequently on relevant topics in family business and family offices. He draws on personal experience from his own family's shipping business to assist clients seeking to resolve complex problems.

Holger Kück has spent the last twelve years building expert, practical knowledge in the world of family office. He has served three families in establishing and operating substantial single family offices, in his native Germany and in Switzerland. After obtaining his diploma in banking, Mr. Kück went on to the University of London, where he earned a masters degree in finance.

Colleen Lief is a research associate working with IMD on family business and corporate culture projects. She earned a master of philosophy in monetary economics from the University of Glasgow and a bachelor of science in business administration from Duquesne University, Pittsburgh. Ms. Lief spent nearly twenty years as a commercial banker at major financial institutions in the U.S.

The Cycle of Wealth

Over the twenty plus years in which IMD has been involved in family business education, we have heard many stories of the struggles faced by families at different points in their life cycle. Succession was the first hot topic. As time moved on, governance and strategy took center stage. Most recently, the role of corporate culture in the life of the firm and family, and how to do a good job at philanthropy and family office, have taken their turn in the spotlight.

But what occurred to us as time went on is that all of these important subjects are elements of one integrated system. You cannot consider one in isolation from the rest. In fact, we came to believe that families in business operate in a cyclical way rather than keeping things in discrete boxes (refer to Figure A). It all generally starts, of course, with one person, a good idea and a passion that will not be denied. While what comes next – family business and family office – represents some of the most complex dynamics, organizations and relationships in the world, these entities are also some of the most successful. Research has proven that, overall, family businesses report superior financial results compared with their non-family peers operating in much less complicated environments. Why and how are questions that have intrigued us. We believe, however, that we are making progress in gaining more insights into enterprising families and how all the pieces fit together.

Wealth creation remains something of a mystery; it happens in some circumstances and yet not in others, which seem equally promising. But there are discernable patterns. The most obvious one is a trend downwards. Failure and losses are more often the rule than the exception in business. In no country is this more evident than in the United States. Business bankruptcy filings are estimated at 15 percent of court filings every year in the U.S.[1] And it is estimated that counting the number of bankruptcies does not even scratch the surface of business failures. Because bankruptcy actions are costly, many businesses in the U.S. simply opt for the more pragmatic Chapter 7 filings – orderly liquidation of debt. In the first nine

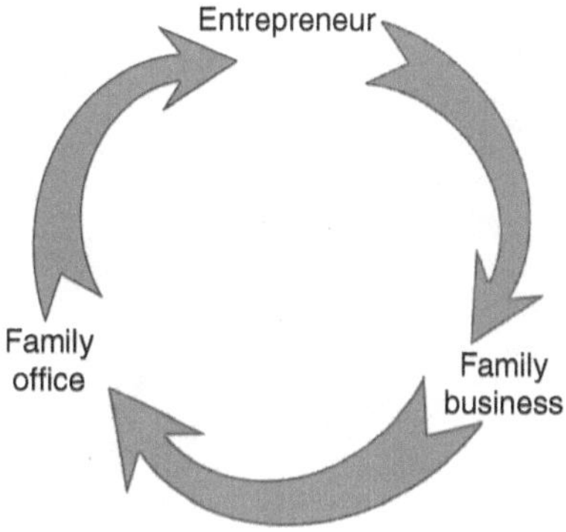

Figure A The cycle of wealth
Source: Joachim Schwass.

months of 2008, 1.15 million companies ceased operations.[2] Having a better understanding of the logic of the wealth creation process raises awareness of the potential risks. Our approach is systems-based and thus leads to a fuller understanding of the process, as well as to an enhanced ability to manage and influence it.

Learning from the most common mistakes and from the most successful entrepreneurs, family businesses and family offices is at the heart of this book. Our mission as authors is to help you plan and execute to make success a reality for your family.

In the rest of the book, we will present our conviction that, as the family moves from entrepreneurship to family business to family office and back to entrepreneurship, change is not the only constant. Structures, processes, rules and culture unique to each family guide its strategies and decisions every step of the way, and this is reflected in a "rules of the road" section at the end of every chapter. The family's philosophy and purpose must remain firm, yet malleable throughout the life cycle. For families that stagnate or do not truly believe in anything of substance, the business quickly perishes. But adherence to a small core set of beliefs and practices, while the family and business remain open to new ideas, can keep them strong and healthy for the long term.

Joachim Schwass, Håkan Hillerström,
Holger Kück, Colleen Lief

1
The Cycle of Entrepreneurship

> We succeed in enterprises which demand the positive qualities we possess, but we excel in those which can also make use of our defects.
>
> —Alexis de Tocqueville[1]

They say there are many roads to both success and disaster. This book will chart the course toward success – a route with lots of opportunities for twists, turns and dead ends – trodden by that highly individualistic creature, the entrepreneur. There is something inside the entrepreneur that will not be denied. He or she is driven by the great urgency of a new idea that no one else has yet conceived and by an unquenchable need for self-expression and independence.

As hard as it is, starting one's own business may be the easiest step in what we think of as the cycle of entrepreneurship or wealth. If a start-up company is successful, it survives and grows and may become a family business if the next generation gets involved. The creativity, passion and deep need to create something out of nothing, which are necessary preconditions for founding a company, are put to the test in the next phase. One reason, among many, that it gets more complicated is that the same qualities that produced success in a solo enterprise may not be the key to making a full-fledged business thrive.

Then you introduce the concept of successors, heirs or whatever you want to call these much loved but often deeply feared offspring. Family business founders seem both proud and apprehensive about involving their children in their business. On the one hand, they may want to share with their children the thing that has been the center of their lives. And passing the company along to the next generation can be a way of ensuring that the firm endures and stands as a testament to the founder. On the other hand, founders are frequently scared that their children might destroy the object of their desire. Certainly business history is peppered with stories of second generation sons who lost the family fortune. So what's a trailblazer to do?

Sometimes they sell before their children can run their baby into the ground. But more often they happily find that their children have imperceptibly picked up knowledge about and an interest in the business, usually around the dinner table and through quiet example. Almost naturally, the second generation seems to have learned how to run the business in harmony with its community, how to run it efficiently together, how to operate effectively over a long-term horizon, how to think about employees, how to make sure the core values it runs on reflect those important to the family, how to handle discord and incongruence in business and family – in short, how to achieve balance, authenticity and their own brand of success in two realms as different as business and family.

Family business

Family business, particularly as the generations roll on, can become highly complex, not only in matters of business strategy but also in relationships. As we will explore further in Chapter 3, the primary reason family businesses fail is the inability of family members to find an effective way to work together for the good of the firm and of the family. Some families try to limit the damage that family relationships can inflict on the business by opting for the single-heir succession, in which a single owner is chosen from each generation. Other families, believing in democracy and in themselves, install an equal ownership plan, such that shares in the company are divided evenly among all members of one generation. Each method has its drawbacks and benefits. In this context, the complicated nature of a concept that is as seemingly straightforward as ownership gives some insight into the complexity of the family business system as a whole. It is a wonder that family firms ever build buildings, make products or succeed at retailing, with everything else going on behind the scenes.

Yet somehow they do all these things, and some do them brilliantly. But what are the key factors that enable family firms to succeed? We are about to find out.

All our research and discussions with business families point to three factors: family and business culture; governance; and a deep connection to purpose. These concepts are all interwoven. Valuing and validating one's own history and agreeing on core values and purpose result in a comprehensive approach that seems to spring from each family uniquely according to its experiences, religion, national origin, language and social context. Constant communication, respect for the independence of the individual, and agreement on the underlying foundations of the business and family almost compel the establishment of exceptional governance structures and of processes that lead to the development of fair rules of the road; and these, in turn, continually breathe new life into the family culture, which forms the basis of everything.

Once the family, and by extension the business, knows why it exists and agrees on how it wishes to conduct itself, the next challenge is operationalizing this ethos to achieve success. If a company is to have a chance at longevity, it must adjust to the times but stay true to certain core doctrines. Some commercial principles, of course, are common to any well-run firm. But others are unique to the family and company and constitute its "DNA." This unique set of principles gives shape to values that form the basis of governance policies and structures; and these can help a family in business navigate the turbulent waters between founder's company and family business and, if it has made it that far, family office and beyond.

Family office

The family office is another manifestation of the family's philosophy. It is a complex and uniquely personal organization, established to serve families and extend their philosophy in the world. Family offices can perform a panoply of functions, from investment management to philanthropy to family education to concierge services. A family office can be formed as a result of the sale of the family business. More often, it is an entity that is separate from the operating business and designed to serve the family's tangible needs: it makes it work in the community and it helps in keeping together a growing group. It can also be a forum for family members to find expression and utility, in furthering family goals, even for skill sets that lie outside of those required in the business. Family members not involved in managing the business may run the group's philanthropic endeavors, ensure the education of the next generation or lead family governance bodies.

Entrepreneurship again

The cycle concludes and begins again when next generation family members find encouragement and, often, tangible financial and emotional support for their latent entrepreneurial talent. Many family offices encourage family members not directly involved in the existing family business to explore their own entrepreneurial side. The chances are good that rugged individualism and creativity have been passed down through the genes to some of the founder's descendants. Their aspirations may not be expressed in the same form as the patriarch's, but smart families provide a forum for the ideas of individual family members to be validated and given wings. Like everything else in successful families, the process can be rigorous. Proposals for new ventures are often made to a committee comprised of family and non-family professionals, which then decides whether or not to support the family member in the fledgling enterprise, and under what terms. Then, like any other portfolio item, the performance of the investment is periodically assessed. This sort of incubator for entrepreneurial talent seems natural to business families; it completes and restarts the cycle of entrepreneurship.

The intriguing part is that the situation, issues and challenges facing a company founder, a family business and a family office could not be more different – or more similar. Everything in the time frame, operating environment and key players is different from one stage to another. But, underpinning each stage in the cycle, there is a collective sense of "who we are, what we believe in and what we do." These deep beliefs are expressed through and supported by structures, processes, rules and a set of values, or culture – the family's DNA brought to life. Each element is essential and inextricable from the others. Nothing can be done very successfully for very long without structures, processes and rules. Without values as the bedrock, however, no structure in the world can be sustaining. At the end of each chapter we will be exploring how structures, processes, rules and culture are expressed at each stage.

In summary, the system we are describing seems to us to represent different manifestations of the singular quality of responsible leadership. At the entrepreneurial stage, everything is about personal leadership. In the family business, family and business objectives and collective leadership come to the fore. This stage is more about teamwork, governance and respect for the individual. In the family office, the concepts of continuity, long-term wealth management and social leadership are more readily in evidence. These varying dimensions of leadership seem to be different ways to express "what we believe" at various stages in the life cycle of a successful family business. So the life of families in business is complex and simple. This may sound confusing to most, but just about right to those born into a business family.

Rules of the road

- Structures: The platform for success and family cohesion is established early, with the founder. It must be nurtured, however, to stay vibrant and operable. Structures may change, but values stay the same at each stage of the cycle.
- Process: Everything in the system is evolutionary. No sudden changes. Process trumps outcomes.
- Rules: Agree on rules before you need them, and this applies to the process of self-regulation, which your family adopts as well.
- Culture/DNA: Vision and a deep connection to purpose permeate everything. There is no substitute for this. Truly understanding family values and dynamics helps avoid trouble. This takes a good measure of maturity and deep thought. Some families' cultures will be unable to sustain a family office.

2
Generation One – The Entrepreneur

> Nothing in the world can take the place of persistence. Talent will not; nothing is more common than successful men with talent. Genius will not; unrewarded genius is almost a proverb. Education alone will not; the world is full of educated derelicts. Persistence and determination alone are omnipotent.
>
> —Calvin Coolidge[1]

Let's face it, entrepreneurs are a special breed. They find fulfillment in making their unique mark on the world. Working in someone else's firm would simply not offer the opportunity for self-expression that coming up with an idea and running with it could. At their own company, they know they are architect-in-chief.

Not that launching a new enterprise is all plain sailing. Choppy seas in both life and commerce are to be expected. Some notable entrepreneurs believe that the hard times not only can be successfully weathered, but also may offer some of the greatest lessons in business. They can be extremely valuable in learning about one's most important asset – oneself. Steve Jobs and his partner, Steve Wozniak, started Apple Computer in 1976. Yet by 1985, and after contributing much to the company's growth and earning many plaudits, Jobs was asked to leave. He floundered around for awhile, trying to figure out what to do next. He realized he loved what he did and helped start NeXT Software and Pixar, which were ultimately, and ironically, acquired by Apple. Jobs credits the humbling experience of being fired from Apple and the soul-searching that followed with unlocking one of the most creative and life-affirming periods of his career. Most importantly, he recognized the depth of his love of the computing and technology fields.[2]

When starting a firm from scratch, it is up to the founder not only to design its more tangible elements, such as strategic direction and manufacturing and marketing plans, but also, and even more importantly, to imbue the organization with the philosophy, culture and character it will need to have in order to survive. The entrepreneur's leadership style and seriousness of purpose must be powerful enough to bring together an enthusiastic group of people and motivate them to join in a common, untried endeavor.

Leading a first-generation organization begins with the entrepreneur's very personal characteristics and values. How someone will lead an organization is, of necessity, significantly influenced by his or her own personal code for living, which is extended to the company. How could it be otherwise?

True power in organizations emanates from the personal demonstration of capabilities, persuasiveness, relationship competencies, curiosity, openness and respect, as well as from the capacity to communicate effectively. Leading by example and demonstrating what you believe in, living it every day, conveys an optimistic, life-affirming message. It says to the world, "We are about something." A company based on values implies "a faith in some transcendent good"[3] and signals that the organization is pursuing its own self-directed path. By implication, an authentic, but not necessarily perfect, philosophy underpins the culture of the corporation.

What makes an entrepreneur?

The entrepreneur is a special breed: part adventurer, part benefactor, part genius, part misfit, part fool. Fear of failure is often a trait. The words ambitious, humble, authentic, risk-taking, driven, resilient, hard-working and modest are often associated with founders. Some of these characteristics could be said to be in opposition to others, but the seeming contradiction is not a problem for either founders or the enterprising families that follow them. Obviously, entrepreneurs' individual philosophies will vary and will contain inconsistencies and personal shortcomings. The set of values they hold dear may appear counterintuitive, but their complete dedication to what they believe in is never in question.

Entrepreneurs seem to develop a world view early on, and to believe that they know how things work, or how they should work. Their quest for independence, with perhaps a tinge of idealism, propels them forward, into unknown territory. They possess a unique vision of the world and of themselves. They have the means and often the desire to improve people's lives and to expand the prevailing ideas of what is possible. They have the ability to view situations differently from other people.

For example, in the 1980s, when the Swiss watch industry was under threat from cheaper quartz watches made in Japan and Hong Kong, Nicolas Hayek stepped in with a unique solution[4] to the problem of mass market competition. He realized that the advent of technology that made inexpensive watches highly dependable required Swiss manufacturers to differentiate themselves in another way. The marketing emphasis would be the timepiece as a statement of taste. As CEO from 1985 to 2003, Hayek consolidated the production processes of eighteen brands under the Swatch Group. The centerpiece of the new company was the Swatch, a sleek, fashionable watch sold at modest prices. By taking a comprehensive view of branding, manufacturing and global competitive market realities, Hayek came up with a response that saved the Swiss watch industry.

Visionary leaders

Responsible leadership is highly personal. We believe that one can develop leadership qualities, but that such qualities cannot be created where they do not exist. The basic assumption of management education in previous years, that good leaders can be made, is flawed. Without the right philosophy, the innate skills and the basic raw materials, a person cannot be magically transformed into a responsible leader. Training can only do so much.

The leader is critical to the firm, but so are the employees he leads and their characteristics. The founder needs others to bring life and action to his vision. He needs to identify colleagues who complement his talents as well as fitting in with his personality.

Are family business employees different from non-family company employees? In general, yes – absolutely. If the selection process is done right, family business employees are hired into the company already sharing the beliefs of the firm. Through their own personal experiences, employees have independently developed a philosophy that dovetails with that of the firm. As failed corporate initiatives focusing on convincing staff to buy into management philosophy have shown in the past, no one will convince another of a personal code for living. That is why selection is so critical. Uncovering more than just a candidate's professional skills set is tricky but necessary. Some competencies may be acquired through training; deeply held beliefs cannot.

The bottom line is that leadership is a system. The leader, followers and context all contribute to whether things get done, and how. That is why family firms are miles ahead of their non-family peers in almost every respect we can measure. By and large, business families have given themselves license to step back and see the big picture of what really makes a company, workforce and community tick. It is the combination of the principles the company was founded on, reinterpreted and made relevant for the current day, that forms the DNA that is the true differentiator.

Are entrepreneurs born or made?

This is an eternal question, which is still being debated. From our own experience, we can point to evidence in favor of both sides of the alternative. Research done by Scott Shane at Case Western Reserve University concluded that entrepreneurs are 40 percent born and 60 percent made.[5] It seems reasonable to say that recognizing optimal business conditions or product ideas can be the result of either a tendency passed along within families or a response to one's environment and experiences – or maybe of both.

Context can be a key factor in whether the latent qualities in entrepreneurs are developed or not. Serendipitous opportunities (either emerging or actively sought) can provide a platform for the entrepreneur to live up to his potential. Two key issues for any entrepreneur, though, are risk and passion.

Risk

To become an entrepreneur means overcoming risks and barriers of all types. It is often said that the biggest risk is not to take any risk. In class at the Swiss business school IMD, Master of Business Administration (MBA) students were asked what they considered to be the most important risks when contemplating becoming an entrepreneur. They identified three key levels of risk:

- Personal: Fear of failure
    - Sense of insecurity
    - Lack of personal skills
    - Lack of financial resources
    - Lack of family support
- Professional: Leaving a secure job
    - Lacking business skills
    - Peer pressure
- Contextual: Lack of opportunities

Successful entrepreneurs often note that too much focus and too much rationalizing on risks is unhealthy for the entrepreneurial process. Assessing and evaluating risks provide rational information and data which need to be counterbalanced by more emotionally driven aspirations and dreams of success.

Passion

The primary emotional factor contributing to commitment, excellence and, finally, success is passion. This emotion is evident in the words of Salvatore Ferragamo, dubbed "Shoemaker to the Stars," who had set up his own shoe shop in Bonito, Italy, by the age of 13, rebuilt his business following bankruptcy in the wake of the Wall Street crash of 1929, and prided himself on the proper fit of the shoes he made:

> I love feet – they talk to me. As I take them into my hands, I feel their strengths, their weaknesses, their vitality or their failings. A good foot, its muscles firm, its arch strong, is a delight to touch, a masterpiece of divine workmanship. A bad foot is an agony. As I take those feet in my hands, I am consumed with anger and compassion – anger that I cannot shoe all the feet in the world, compassion for all those who walk in torment.[6]

Intangibles are at the heart of why people embark on an uncertain path and start their own business (see Figure 2.1).

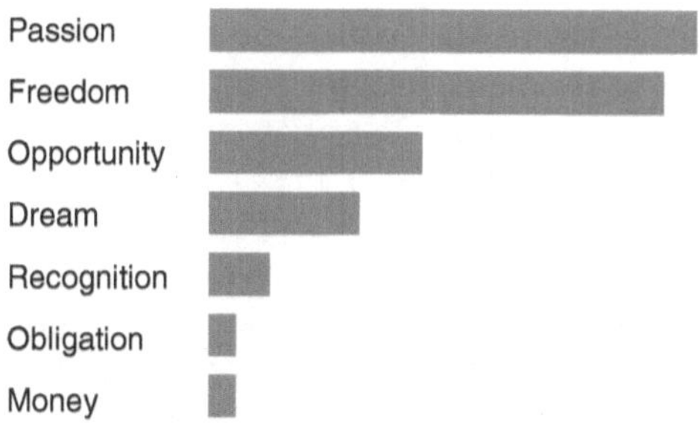

Figure 2.1 Reasons for starting a new business
Source: Survey of 40 entrepreneurs (1–10 years' experience), *Créateurs*, NO. 30, June 2004: 8–9.

Passion is without doubt the key driving force. It may not always be there at the beginning and it may not always be explicit, yet it sustains the extraordinary efforts of successful entrepreneurs. We have identified three important types of passion:

- Product passion
- People passion
- Values passion

Product passion is the typical driving force in the first and founding generation, as expressed by Salvatore Ferragamo. Fritz Henkel, founder of the Henkel chemical products group in Germany, developed detergents for use in individual households. In a quest to provide customers with a quality guarantee, he launched the first branded detergent product in 1907 under the name of Persil, which remained the market leader in Germany for over a hundred years.

People passion drives entrepreneurs to team efforts. They are motivated by jointly pursuing an objective and constructing something together, in partnership. The underlining dynamics are "pull and push." The complementarity works on a rational knowledge-and-skills level and, in addition, on a more emotional level of mutual encouragement. Today start-ups are increasingly undertaken by teams. However, few teams survive the pressures of entrepreneurship.

A passion for values is driven by deep-seated convictions, and is often expressed as a need to address and rectify what is perceived to be unjust. Social, environmental and ecological causes are increasingly espoused and furthered by entrepreneurs. Today this is more explicit than in the past – one can hardly open a newspaper or listen to the news without seeing or hearing phrases like "climate change" or "corporate social responsibility." These were far less "fashionable" concepts in 1932, when Ermenegildo Zegna, the second-generation leader of the eponymous company, started building hospitals and schools in Trivero, northern Italy, as well as embarking on the reforestation of local mountain slopes with 500,000 conifers, rhododendrons and hydrangeas. His son called his father "an ecologist, well before the word existed."[7]

Passions can change over time. Especially during generational transitions, much attention needs to be devoted to allowing the successors to identify and pursue their own passion. Product passion can be difficult to transmit. Some successors have told us that, although they admire the founder's passion for the firm's products, they do not necessarily share it. This is particularly obvious for basic products like nuts and bolts! It is then that successors need to reflect on what might motivate them best to move forward. In later generations, the values passion typically becomes a strong driving force.

The environment as a factor

It is not only the individual that plays a role in entrepreneurship. Have you ever noticed that many of the world's great and long-lived companies were founded at specific periods in history? It makes sense that certain points in time may be catalysts or facilitators for budding entrepreneurs. Three specific periods stand out:

The free trade era

As the nineteenth century gave way to the twentieth, a number of enduring family businesses got their start: Henkel, the German adhesive, laundry and beauty products firm; S.C. Johnson, the U.S. manufacturer of household products; Bata, the shoe company headquartered in Switzerland; Murugappa Group, the Indian conglomerate; Ford Motor Company, the global automobile manufacturer; Lee Kum Kee, the Hong Kong-based condiment producer; and the Italian fashion house, Ermenegildo Zegna, among others. Companies founded in this period can be seen as a link between the capital-intensive industries of the nineteenth century and the consumer-led markets later in the twentieth century.[8] The concept of "survival of the fittest" gained traction, ushering in a period in which success was seen to be a matter of determination and science rather than inherited wealth or distinguished lineage.[9] These ideas took the guilt out of wealth accumulation by asserting that riches were deserved; and they laid the groundwork for the capitalism of the twentieth century.

Free trade and an integrated international economy were potent factors at the dawn of the twentieth century. The gold standard provided stability to the economic system and so supported the many advances in industry occurring in this era.[10]

The post-war era

Firms founded after World War II include tool manufacturer Hilti, based in Liechtenstein; the Israeli producer of machine tools Iscar (now part of Berkshire Hathaway); one of the world's largest companies, Wal-Mart, based in Arkansas; the shipbuilders Klaveness Group of Norway; the clothing store H&M and the furniture and home accessory store IKEA, both of Sweden. All of these firms benefited from renewed optimism and a need for high quality goods and services following World War II.

The post-war period opened up the four corners of the globe to technology and innovative ideas. Scientific progress gave rise to new pharmaceutical and computer businesses.[11] And the world needed all the engineering, heavy industry and cutting-edge technologies that had been given life during the war to help the reconstruction effort, once hostilities ceased.

The technological boom era

In the 1970s and 1980s, the economy was profoundly influenced by deregulation and modern era trust busting. At the same time financial innovations, previously unimagined technologies and drastic advances in communication began to have a profound impact. The moribund corporations of the 1960s were led to a slow death by their own bureaucracies and huge size.

The result of all this was that companies began to value flexibility as much as size, and innovation as much as their bread-and-butter manufacturing systems. In turn, the new technologies and approaches to business brought product development closer to the customer, enabling even more sophisticated marketing efforts. When, in the late twentieth century, this more integrated system of commerce was combined with supportive U.S. Federal Reserve moves and stock market innovations like the mass marketing of merger and acquisitions; and initial public offering transactions, business and entrepreneurship really came into its own.[12]

The latter part of the century saw the creation and flourishing of innovative companies such as Microsoft, Yahoo!, Apple, Virgin, Black Entertainment Television, SAP, Infosys, Skype and Google. The General Infantry Bill of Rights in the U.S. may have contributed to this generation of entrepreneurs by establishing higher education as the societal norm,[13] thereby paving the way for the development of more sophisticated technologies.

The darker side of entrepreneurship

"Life is lonely at the top." We've all heard this saying, and it is true that with power and wealth comes pressure of various kinds. Isolation not only can impact an entrepreneur's growing business, but also needs to be dealt with on a personal level. Divorce, illness and excesses of different sorts can manifest themselves. Describing Konosoke Matsushita, founder of the $65 billion Matsushita Electric Corporation, John Kotter notes:

> The public persona was a great businessman who often behaved like a saint. The private side included screaming, sleeping pills, and a mistress. Deeper than both was a tornado of emotions that came to be directed by a set of beliefs and convictions that are difficult for the skeptic in all of us to comprehend.[14]

Personal qualities and consequences aside, taking on the mantle of entrepreneurship implies an additional set of constraints and implications for the company. Once you incorporate, or otherwise declare yourself a business entity, a whole host of legal and financial imperatives come to bear. Things you never thought about when you dreamed up that big idea. In the words of Ivar Kreuger, the so-called Match King, who built his fortune on the Swedish safety match:

> Today the world demands balance sheets, profit-and-loss statements once a year. But if you're really working on great ideas, you can't supply these on schedule and expose yourself to view. Yet

> you've got to tell the public something, and so long as it's satisfied and continues to have faith in you, it's really not important what you confess. And some day people will realize that every balance sheet is wrong because it doesn't contain anything but figures. The real strengths and weaknesses of an enterprise lie in the plans.

Convinced that his way of doing business would prove him right at the end, Kreuger found himself cornered during the financial crisis of 1929. He had personally falsified Italian government bonds to the value of $100 million, using them as collateral. This is one example of a driven and passionate entrepreneur who struggled with boundaries – legal and moral. Entrepreneurs often find it difficult to accept checks and balances, which are alien to the "revolutionary" change on which they are embarking.

It is important to understand the external and internal tensions entrepreneurs experience. These tensions are one reason why most start-ups fail. And they are also the reason why succeeding generations of highly successful entrepreneurs are surprised when they discover "darker" sides to the founder as a person.

The cycle of entrepreneurship begins

Throughout this book we will see how the philosophies, practices and processes that find their start with the founding generation persist in some form throughout the rest of the life of the firm and family. Each stage has its own dynamics and operating characteristics.

At the entrepreneurial stage, the business, at first, has only one employee – the founder. Even when the staff inevitably grows larger, the number of owners will still be one. Since decisions will be made by the owner, it seems natural that the prevailing power orientation would emphasize control. The culture revolves around the "I" that led the founder to establish his own business in the first place. The company is the ultimate expression of self. As described earlier, the main capital at work in the fledgling enterprise is the power of the entrepreneur's personality. Everything springs from his sense of self, world view, competencies and past experiences. Finally, the type of change underway is fundamental, revolutionary. To create something where nothing existed is the ultimate act of a revolution.

We have discussed how entrepreneurs have drive, ambition and a firm belief in themselves and their company. They utilize the full range of their personal qualities, both positive and negative, to push their idea from theory to reality. Since the founder sets the whole system in motion, it makes sense that processes, structures, rules, culture and everything else in the company are set up in his image and are often based on a rather utopian foundation. The firm reflects the founder's personality and character, as well as his idea of how the world can work. The basis on which the firm is established will set the tone for all that comes after, as we will see in the next chapters.

Case in point: The Owens family

Richard Owens had a dream. And in 1906 he realized it. Richard took a gamble and used his savings and some lottery winnings to purchase a general store in rural Australia. The store thrived through service excellence born of Richard's previous experience in the retail industry. He was determined that, if he ever had a store of his own, it would be based on trust, respect and putting the customer first.

He soon realized, however, that customer service would not be enough to keep the business flying high, and a single location did not fulfill his vision of an Owens family business. He expanded to another city and continued his commitment to the customer and to the communities in which he worked. His sons and wife worked alongside him in the business.

While Richard included his wife and children in his vision, he did not include them in the ownership of what was now Richard Owens Pty. Ltd. Richard's family was awarded non-voting shares and shared in the profits. The business expanded further, with the launch of a grocery wholesaling company. Richard's concept of family responsibility and profit without control would be tested by his sudden death in 1929.

Rules of the road for entrepreneurs

- Structures: At the start, there are no structures. It is just trial and error and experimentation. But, once a critical size and workable base have been achieved, structures are needed. However, often the entrepreneur is not good at building structures and nurturing them. You need to rely on others. Structures put in place early on will change over time, but the overall rationale for the company's governance and organization will persist. Make sure your approach is solid and well considered and fully reflects your ethos.

- Process: The system starts with a revolutionary act. Everything that follows is incremental. Encourage innovation and welcome failure as an opportunity to learn.
- Rules: Establish rules that respect the individual and the many freedoms that permitted you to found a business of your own. Your heirs will thank you. Recognize when it is time to become the coach and let others take the baton.
- Culture/DNA: Dedication and unity of purpose trump faux sophisticated management theories every day of the week. The first generation constructs the vision and applies values which define the unique imprint (what we have called the DNA), thus impacting future generations.

3
Generation Two and Beyond – The Family Business

> My favorite child has always been the business.
>
> —Heard from a surprisingly large number of family business owners

What exactly is a family business? There is no simple answer to this question. In family business research, many varied definitions are used to describe companies with concentrated ownership – that is, companies that are concentrated in the hands of one or more families (as opposed to companies with dispersed ownership). Some believe a family member must be involved in day-to-day management for the business to qualify as a family company; others say that merely having influence over the operation of a firm is enough. We consider a company to be a family business when it has experienced at least one generational transition and is owned by one or more families, such that they exert control over the enterprise. We think this only comes about through holding voting shares equal to at least 30 percent.

Family businesses are different from non-family ones in almost every way. Study after study shows that family firms outperform their peers in profitability. For example, some years ago, Morgan Stanley conducted research on the corporations that constitute the Standard and Poor's (S&P) 500. The study revealed that family businesses within the index outperformed the index itself by 4.4 percent over one year and by 109.7 percent over five years.[1] Similarly, research carried out by Oddo Asset Management in September 2009 found that the results of family and non-family firms engaged in the same industries – public relations and tire manufacturing – differed meaningfully. Over one year ending in September 2009, the family companies reported better growth in revenues (or rather less of a loss), operating margins and stock market performance.[2]

And, while naysayers often point out how many family companies disappear before the third generation takes over, the average life of a firm with dispersed ownership does not fare much better. Family businesses also play a major role in the world's economic landscape, accounting for a major portion of gross domestic product (GDP) in the U.S. and many European countries. And a Harvard Law School study found that, among companies in the S&P 500 from 1992 to 2004, the tenure of the average family business chief executive officer (CEO) (holding over 1 percent of company shares) was 13.4 years, compared with 5.5 for non-family firms.[3] Other research backs up this disparity by noting that the global tenure of non-family business CEOs lasts a mere 7.8 years.[4]

The previous paragraphs outline how prominently family enterprises figure in the world economy. But what makes family firms able to achieve these heights of success and social contribution is their many differences, by comparison with publicly listed companies run by hired hands. At the heart of it, family enterprises have a completely different set of motivations and strategic approaches. These companies are focused on the preservation of the assets and philosophy passed on to them. Even more importantly, the notion of stewardship, generally ingrained in family business owners, requires that they must not only protect but also sustainably grow family assets and provide leadership to the next generation, so that it may do the same when its turn comes.

Family businesses emphasize incremental over explosive growth, evolutionary over revolutionary change; they have an eye to both the future and the past. The time horizon that these companies consider in their planning is gauged in decades, not in quarters. A distinctive feature of concentrated ownership is that, although the company is held by a relatively small group of so-called "principals," the latter see their constituencies in much wider terms than most businesses. In the world of family business, the community, staff, environment, suppliers, regulators and others are included as stakeholders.

How is it possible for family companies to face the same challenges as every other firm, plus the complications that we all know accompany family, and still excel? Perhaps the answer is that balancing family and business does not detract from the system but rather enhances it. Even if this sounds rather far-fetched, it is what is occurring every day in family firms all over the globe.

Who you are contributes to your success

All the apparent gymnastics inherent in a family business system is more than a mere complication. It is integral to family business success. Some years ago, we looked at family business performance and asked ourselves what it really was that made family businesses outperform their peers, in spite of the many obstacles. The answer? Culture.

As mentioned in Chapter 2, a distinctive approach to people, stakeholders and the world is set in motion by the founder. It is only natural that the heirs of this unique person, carrying at least some of his philosophies, beliefs – and shortcomings – in their genes, would sustain the personalized culture in the family and firm, albeit with the imprint of their own personalities and experiences.

The quality and style of leadership, the employees and the strength of the corporate culture are crucial to family companies staying in business and allowing the vision of the founder to live. So matters of human resources, how the workspace reflects company philosophy, and other issues often relegated to the back burner in companies with dispersed ownership take on particular meaning in a family firm. Being true to the founder's ideals is important to his or her children and also to the culture bearers who worked for that person.

In order for the company to remain intact and be a testament to the founder, the transmission of cultural values must be achieved across time and generations. Responsible leadership is crucial in facilitating this: Emotionally intelligent leaders take a different approach to strategy, people and management and touch all parts of the company and family, helping to ensure continuity. The job becomes harder as the years wear on, as the rising needs of a growing family challenge the firm. But capable family leadership must ensure the continuity of the company as a platform for family unity, wealth and culture.

Cultural archetypes of family businesses

Our research has identified three cultural archetypes of family businesses: ephemeral, preserving and entrepreneurial. Ephemeral businesses, as the name suggests, do not survive for very long, typically failing in the early stages of the second generation, or even of the first. This is usually because there is no vision or effective system for ownership transition. This happens frequently with smaller companies, but larger ones are not immune either. Parmalat, the dairy giant in Italy, is a notable example of a large company that faced bankruptcy because the founder did not have a sustainable, values-based mission. Similarly, the financial investment firm Madoff in New York, run by the founder and other members of the family, including his sons, could be described as ephemeral. Clearly, a lack of values – honesty in particular – led to the demise of the family business in the first generation.

Preserving family firms have typically been going for several generations, adopting a safeguarding strategy to perpetuate the business. The Hénokiens is a Paris-based association of forty very old family businesses from around the world. Member firms are from a variety of sectors and have to be at least 200 years old and financially sound. The majority are owned and managed by the founder's descendants (see Table 3.1 for some examples).

Clearly one reason for these firms' survival is that they are active in industries which will always be in demand: food, drink, travel, trading, banking, and the like. Furthermore, many of them rely on close interaction with key stakeholders, especially clients. Being anchored in local, regional communities gives them stability, visibility and valuable contacts. Trust has been built up over generations. Deep product and process knowledge has been passed on from generation to generation. Many of them possess real estate assets, which give

Table 3.1 The Hénokiens

Year founded	Family business	Country
717	Hoshi Hotel	Japan
1321	Coussergues Wines	France
1526	Beretta Firearms	Italy
1637	Gekkeikan Sake	Japan
1639	Hugel & Fils Wines	France
1662	Van Eeghen Merchant	Holland
1783	Confetti Pelino	Italy

each generation roots. It is a fact that physical assets – land and buildings – require continuity in planning and often impose their own discipline on owning families.

Perhaps the most interesting insight from this group of distinguished family businesses is that many of them are not very large. The Hoshi Hotel in Komatsu is a 46th generation family business with just one hotel, with 100 rooms. This goes against conventional wisdom and general management theory that, "if a business does not grow, it dies." Private wealth and ownership allows a family to design the strategy and culture it wants, as long as the business model is viable. This approach has two implications – the company must have:

- Concentrated ownership and, ideally, an owner/manager in each generation. This eventuality cannot be taken for granted and needs to be planned.
- No or low financial leverage.

The third cultural archetype is that of a family business with an entrepreneurial culture. These are the ones that have provided us with many of our important insights. At the business school IMD they have been the backbone of more than two decades of our research and educational activities around the globe. In 1996, together with Lombard Odier – a family business of private bankers founded in 1796 in Geneva – IMD launched the Global Family Business Award to acknowledge family enterprises that have successfully blended family and business interests. The award highlights best practices and innovative solutions for specific family business management issues. Winners are great examples of an entrepreneurial, yet sustainable, corporate and family culture (see Table 3.2). They are not the biggest, nor necessarily the most profitable, but they all assume a focused, adaptive and balanced approach and pass it along to future generations.

One distinguishing factor of this group of family businesses is their "enlightened" leadership. Typically their leaders reflect on the future of the family as owners of businesses. They educate themselves to appreciate better their specific challenges and to initiate a carefully planned development process. This usually starts with a structured understanding of the opportunities and obstacles implicit in family business.

Table 3.2 Entrepreneurial family businesses: IMD-Lombard Odier Award winners

Year of award	Company	Country
1996	LEGO	Denmark
1997	Hermès	France
1998	Puig	Spain
1999	Henkel	Germany
2000	Zegna	Italy
2001	Murugappa Group	India
2002	S.C. Johnson	United States
2003	Bonnier	Sweden
2004	Barilla	Italy
2005	Votorantim	Brazil
2006	Fundació Lluís Carulla	Spain
	Ivey Foundation	Canada
	Lopez Group Foundation	The Philippines
2007	Yazaki	Japan
2008	Roca Corporación Empresarial	Spain
2009	Merck (Germany)	Germany
2010	Odebrecht	Brazil

Striking a balance

Family firms are constantly weighing family concerns versus business concerns. If this balance is not managed properly, each world can add to or detract from the agenda of the other. Sometimes the two systems work together to create something great. More often, they work diametrically to create something even better. The push–pull of the system seems to give it energy and gravitas.

But, make no mistake, family and business are in no way similar, as reflected in Figure 3.1. Families are systems characterized by feelings, a sense of fair play and an air of permanence. A family can be understood as a more "socialist"-oriented structure, one that is needs-based and often entitlement-driven. Business, by contrast, is a capitalist system thriving on rational thinking and on a belief in meritocracy – all within the limited time frame of the next quarter.

We have recognized that the stark contrast between these two systems can produce stunning accomplishments. Being exposed to a system of different and opposing views and having to learn from early on that both are valid provides a great developmental platform

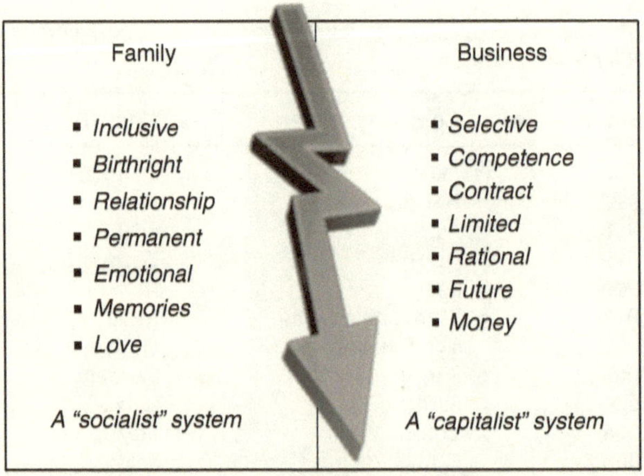

Figure 3.1 Two different systems leading to dilemmas

for learning to embrace complexity. This is not about black-or-white outcomes, but instead about attempting to imagine solutions that have multiple benefits. We often find that family-business members have a greater sense of empathy, reflected in a better understanding of diverse perspectives and in their working towards "win–win" solutions when others might already have given up. But dichotomy of combining family and business can also provide a context for dilemma, conflict and role confusion. The most frequent source of confusion is the transition to the next generation, which may feel entitled – by birthright – to a role in the business. On top of this, family business is a living system, constantly evolving. Changes, incremental or monumental, in family or enterprise mean that families not only have to be competent and able to manage competing aims, but they also have to be flexible and forward-thinking.

What comes next

Well, if you are lucky, what comes next after an entrepreneurial start-up is a second-generation family business. The founder passes on management and, often rather begrudgingly, ownership to any number of his children. He or she may decide that a strong single owner has worked so far and will mandate that ownership succession will

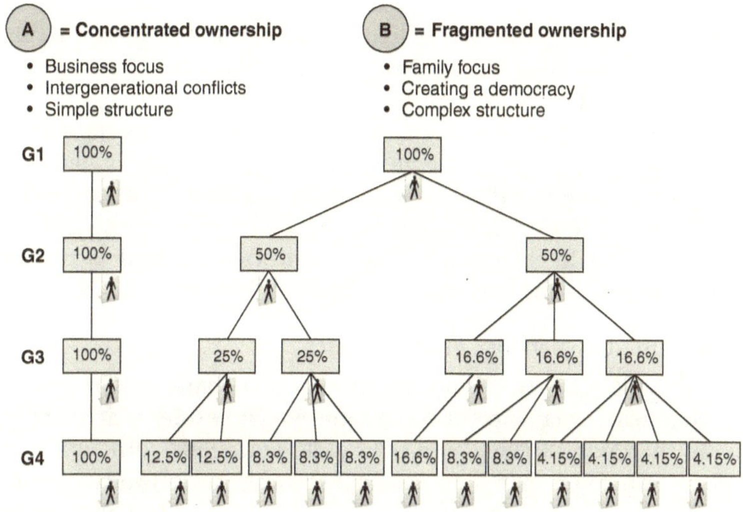

Figure 3.2 Family ownership options

continue to operate in that way, choosing one child to be the sole owner of shares. Nowadays, the choice is more often for equality – that is, for dividing ownership of the business equally among one's heirs. Each of the above approaches brings its own benefits and complications (see Figure 3.2).

Concentrated ownership: A single heir

The single heir system (Model A) is designed to ensure continuity and to limit infighting among family members, which could threaten the firm. This is the long-established model of primogeniture. Successions in monarchies, as well as in farming communities, have followed this line. The logic is compelling: splitting the farm among a number of inheritors will inevitably, over time, lead to downsizing, inefficiencies and loss of critical mass and, ultimately perhaps, of the business.

The strong point of this system is that the rule is simple, predictable and understood by all. The second born child knows from early on that another career path needs to be found. The weak point of the system is that leadership is not defined by merit and competence.

A further complication arises if the successor is not interested in taking over the business, in which case some families adopt an heir from among closer or more distant relatives.

The business aside, the single heir system can also cause problems in the family as siblings who are shut out of power in the business might fear a loss of influence in the family. They may believe their inheritance is under threat and wonder about the quality of their relationship with their parent. The system can also lead to sibling jealousies and in-fighting.

Fragmented ownership: Multiple heirs

In the fragmented ownership system (Model B), shares are distributed among heirs equally, or in some form which ensures that there is more than one successor/owner in each generation. Although this might seem fairer than having a single heir, it has its own problems. Children may inherit equally, but not all siblings are equally gifted, motivated, interested or educated. Equality brings a whole series of issues bubbling to the surface – for example providing exit opportunities; what to do when shareholders without business know-how involve themselves in decision making; uninterested shareholders not pulling their weight in the governance arena; how each family branch will pass shares to the next generation; and, as the generations progress, how to effect real family influence in the company when shareholdings may have dwindled to extremely small individual portions.

Unlike Model A, which represents the primacy of the business at the expense of a number of family members, Model B attempts to create a long-lasting "marriage" between family and business, by placing more emphasis on family. Family is there to benefit from the wealth that has been created by the previous generation. A strong focus on family governance structures is required here. Since more family members are involved at different levels, rules become a condition of continuity. Who decides what? This is about creating a new democracy from scratch.

Succession planning

Succession is always the most difficult chapter in the life of entrepreneurs, families and their business. Many factors must be considered. Does the business model allow for another generation of family ownership? Can a growing and diverse family adequately add value to the business and benefit from it? How is family harmony affected by increasing ownership inequality over generations? What type of leadership can the next generation bring to the business?

Transitions are a rare event, so families do not get much practice at it, and if a transition involves the most precarious change – that from the founder to the second generation – the people involved have no experience in this realm. Succession is especially hard because it implicitly acknowledges mortality as inevitable.

Mariano Puig Sr. of the Spanish Puig Corporation, owner of brands such as Nina Ricci, Paco Rabanne and Carolina Herrera, provides some deep insights into the mindset of retiring executives:

> When we were getting close to the conclusion, I must admit something happened to me: a strong feeling of hesitation in taking the last step settled in. All of a sudden I had doubts both in regard to [the] economic security of my generation and myself in the future, and also very personal emotional feelings:
>
>> "What will I do the day after my retirement? Will the phone stop ringing? What will be my social identity? Will people say that he is a 'has been?' Always having been active in life and not being a golf player, what will I do every day?"
>
> Very honestly, I experienced feelings of serious doubt about the succession strategy which were bordering on fear![5]

Next-generation members, often pushing hard for control, need to show empathy and understanding for the concern and dilemmas that outgoing leaders face. The risk is high that senior leaders simply postpone retirement and thinking about succession. Research into different types of executive retirement has identified four styles:

- Monarch: Dies on the job or is thrown out
- General: Removed from office and plotting return
- Ambassador: Leaves gracefully and has an advisory role
- Governor: Leaves freely for the next opportunity.[6]

Of course, leaving graciously and promptly can be an emotionally difficult move. In earlier years, especially when the entrepreneur is involved, the Monarch and the General styles seem to be most common. As the family progresses along the continuum, it is to be hoped that the Ambassador and Governor become more prevalent. Family business education and the establishment of strong governance structures can help ensure this is so.

We have found that the best-case scenario for a succession occurs when the outgoing generation has a specific project planned for retirement. In some cases, these projects can be related to the business, for example experimenting with new ideas and concepts away from the business location, now that the members of the new generation have the time to do so, or establishing a commercial outpost for their business in the country to which they retire. Several retiring family business leaders find enjoyment and purpose in tending their own vineyards. The underlying philosophy is that it is better to retire *to* something rather than just retiring *from* something. Individuals are well advised to reflect – early on – on the implications of their retirement and to adopt a proactive strategy, adapted to their own needs and objectives.

Much thought has to be put into the evolving dynamics of intergenerational relationships. Research has shown time and again that this is a difficult period for both the outgoing and the incoming generation. Just as retirement becomes the primary concern of the senior generation, the evolving learning needs and style of the next generation require different responses from the parent generation. At an early age, the "dependent" student requires authority telling him or her the *what*, the *how* and the *who*. Growing up, the now "interested" student requires more motivational support. In the next phase, the "involved" student wishes for a facilitator. And, finally, the now more mature "self-directed" student identifies and defines the knowledge and support needed and freely looks for a competent consultant. We have found that senior generation members too often ignore or underestimate the importance of the evolving needs of the next generation. Increasing emotional distance is the result, frequently leading to inter-generational conflicts.

Evolution of the family business

To help us understand the complex world of family enterprise better, we need to talk about the three-circle model[7] and the worlds of family (F), management (M) and ownership (O).

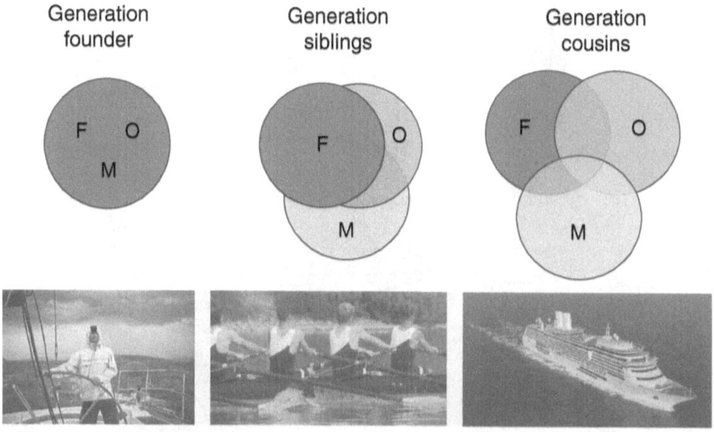

Figure 3.3 Generational evolution of family businesses

This model is a way of encapsulating the notion that each role – family member, manager and owner – carries its own responsibilities, pressures and rewards. For those acting in all three capacities, as many do in the world of family business, the strain can be tremendous. But people who have been raised in business-owning families, although they acknowledge having a full workload, do not think there is anything extraordinary about managing such a diverse set of issues and constituencies. From our research, we believe this comfort with duality is passed imperceptibly to the next generation through example and experiences, which can be as simple as discussions over the dinner table and visiting dad at the office. As Figure 3.3 shows, the situation evolves. Whereas the entrepreneur manages all three facets of his company as sole owner and founder, inevitably, when the business moves to the next generation, roles begin to separate and move according to priorities and group dynamics over time.

First-generation owner/manager

The first generation, at the founder or entrepreneur level, is a simple structure. One individual has full control and power, and creates a new business in a "revolutionary" way. The key asset of the emerging business is the strength, the personality of the founder. This creates an "I" culture: I am family, I own the business and I manage the business. This is the strength of the business model at this stage. But

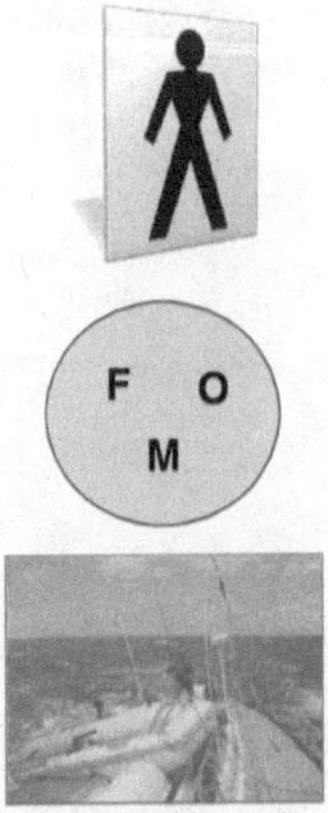

	Founder/ dominant owner
Size	1
Power	Control
Culture	I
Capital	Person(ality)
Change	Revolutionary

Figure 3.4 Generation 1: Owner/manager

it becomes a weakness when the business and the growing family (next generation) tend to outgrow the ability of the founder to add value to a changing business. Succession can go in two directions: the A or the B model of ownership.

The A model, from owner/manager to owner/manager, is about moving from one generation of the "lonely sailor" to another generation of the "lonely sailor" (see Figure 3.4). Personality clashes between generations are predictable as one "I" culture shifts to another, particularly for same gender successions. Cross-gender successions tend to be less competitive and are conducted in a more arm's-length way. We have observed that a succession from father to daughter or from mother to son often tends to be less emotional and competitive. There seems to be a stronger desire for complementarity and effective teamwork. The impact of personality on the business in this model is huge and can be observed in the corporate culture, strategy and governance. Succession, according to the B model of ownership, has other challenges for the next generation of siblings.

Second-generation sibling partnership

In a second-generation sibling partnership, the family has grown to at least two people, thereby doubling the complications. The power base has moved from a control structure to a sharing model, requiring team work. But who will do what, and who will decide? The culture is now about "us" and is centered on competence – who is best suited to which tasks? The emphasis is on taking the firm from a one-man show to the next level. Just as revolutionary thoughts were on the mind of the entrepreneur, so his children seek to apply evolutionary change subtly to improve his creation and keep it fresh. Most frequently, members of the next generation find their own space by improving – but not changing – the business model. The focus is on operational efficiencies and performance. This is a whole new system, to be sure (Figure 3.5).

Second-generation sibling teams are typically strongly committed to a business which they have seen their father or mother build up with great effort and few resources. The attachment to an entrepreneurial culture is still strong. Often better educated than their parents, siblings attempt to bring in more modern management techniques, which are sometimes mistrusted by the senior generation. When two siblings share control, it is not unusual to find a co-CEO structure. A model rarely found in public corporations, it can make great sense in family-owned businesses and it allows siblings to express complementarity and trust in each other. Functional separation is frequently adopted, splitting commercial and

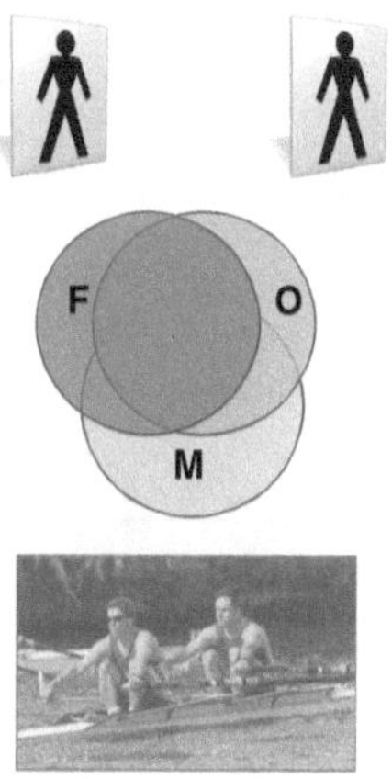

	Siblings
Size	Small family
Power	Sharing
Culture	U.S.
Capital	Competence
Change	Evolutionary

Figure 3.5 Generation 2: Siblings

technical responsibilities. Geographic separation often helps minimize sibling rivalry and competition. Successful siblings share trust through proximity and transparency. The biggest vulnerability occurs when the siblings create new nuclear families by marrying. In-laws often do not understand the complexity of the family business and are mistrustful and jealous of the strong team spirit.

Third-generation cousin consortium

By the time cousins are involved in a family business, there are more discrepancies than before. That is, family members are now of varying ages, genders, nationalities, levels of education and so on. All of this diversity can serve the business well, but may also introduce discord. Certainly the opportunity for confusion and complexity is abundant. The key to understanding power in this phase is to acknowledge that many forces can work to separate not only the family but also, quite often, the roles of family, management and ownership, which can result in an "us and them" mentality (Figure 3.6).

The kinds of changes occurring in both family and business in the third generation and beyond are at once revolutionary and evolutionary, borrowing something from each stage of the collective history. In this phase, ownership and management control tend to be in different hands. The built-in clarity of the previous generations' simplicity is now definitely gone, and governance structures and formal guidelines and procedures are required.

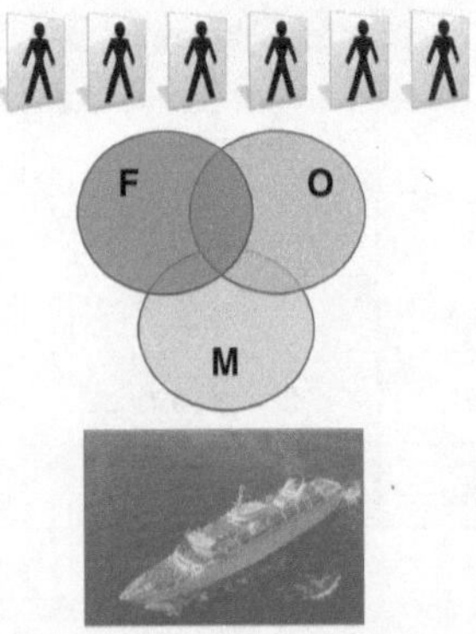

	Cousins
Size	Large family
Power	Separation
Culture	US & THEM
Capital	System
Change	(R)evolutionary

Figure 3.6 Generation 3: Cousins

The third generation frequently arrives at a breakpoint, because the previously unquestioned business model is put under financial strain by family shareholders who are further removed from the once strong emotional family attachment to the business. Financial concerns – actual share value and dividends – are voiced increasingly openly. Passive shareholders may start to question the logic of having often the greater part of their wealth locked up in one business: no liquidity and no risk diversification.

Our research indicates that family businesses are well advised to introduce early exit opportunities, but clearly on terms favorable to the business, including clear valuation formulas, a discount applied to the book value and an extended payout term. The logic is that it may be better to "prune the family ownership tree" in a controlled fashion, in order to preserve a stronger future for the truly committed group of family owners. Often the tension between revolutionary and evolutionary strategies requires a totally new vision for the business to be constructed by the cousin generation.

Paradigm change

As we have seen, there is a constant tension between family and business that needs to be managed, along with the changing roles of family as family member, owner and manager, depending on the generation. The key decision for entrepreneurs – which the vast majority ignore – is how to structure the future of the business beyond their own lifespan. They find it difficult to envision their company without themselves at the helm. Thus the starting point for success is the individual, the founder who passionately, intelligently and energetically creates wealth. It is ironic that the starting point for failure is also the individual – and the family – as the business goes through generational transitions. The changing roles and changing structures require understanding the implications and planning for adaptation.

The evolution of the firm, from founder to sibling partnership to cousin consortium, is summarized in Figure 3.7. It is obvious that generational succession amounts to nothing less than a paradigm change, transitioning from an all-controlling "I" culture to a power-sharing "us" culture. A founder typically dislikes all the attributes of a harmonious team culture which requires taking time to listen

	Founder/ dominant owner	Siblings	Cousins
Size	1	Small family	Large family
Power	Control	Sharing	Separation
Culture	I	US	US & THEM
Capital	Person(ality)	Competence	System
Change	Revolutionary	Evolutionary	(R)evolutionary

Figure 3.7 Generational quantum leaps

to one another's concerns, evaluating pros and cons and aiming for consensus in the decision-making process. The risk is that the next generation of siblings is inadequately prepared for an effective power-sharing structure, since the all-controlling "I" culture is the only approach they have ever experienced. A pertinent example is the India-based Ambani family. The rivalry between the two billionaire brothers exploded after the founder, the richest man in India, died without leaving a will.

Moving from a sibling "us" culture to a cousin "us and them" culture amounts to yet another paradigm change. The cousin structure often brings wide diversity. There are two essential ways to deal with this. First, by "pruning the family ownership tree." Buying out dissenting family members leaves a cohesive group of cousins who share the vision. The second way of dealing with diversity is through a cultural approach whereby the mindset of the family is directed towards an explicit acceptance of diversity. Rather than "punishing" or excluding dissenters, their views are dealt with in a spirit of "it is good to be different." Family members are educated about the benefits of diversity and about differences which can bring greater creativity, knowledge and humility. This cultural mindset is supported by an effective governance structure which provides for clarity of roles and guidelines on how to communicate effectively.

Case in point: The Owens family

Picking up from where we left off with the Owens family in Chapter 2, we find that, although the business had flourished under the strong leadership of the patriarch, Richard, things became more much more uncertain after his death in 1929. Ownership was divided among his wife Tess and his sons – Bill, Arthur and George. Although this structure accurately reflected the founder's vision of equality and responsibility among the siblings, it may have ultimately led to the dissolution of the family and business he was trying so ardently to protect.

In the decades that followed, discord and animosity among the brothers was tangible. They had divergent ideas about strategy, product offerings – and just about everything else. They were very different people. Living under a system that implied they were equally gifted, interested and diligent became a real irritant in family relations. Events really got out of hand when Tess died. She was the glue that had held the family together.

Without the leavening influence of Tess, the brothers proceeded to let their personal animosities negatively impact the business. These non-productive tendencies came to a head when each brother wanted to bring his children into the business, almost to spite the others (see Appendix A).

George's son, Richard, had shown great promise in his own career as a pharmacist. But he was drafted into the family company when his father suffered from complications of overwhelming stress. Richard seemed to take to the business naturally, and became its leader in short order. He effectively led the company and was a board member, along with his father and two uncles. However, the rivalries of the second generation emerged anew, as the brothers sought equal treatment, pay and board representation for their children, regardless of their contribution to the company's success.

(Continued)

Richard finally had to issue an ultimatum to the other directors. They had to recognize and resolve the problems that had built up over many years, starting with their resignations from the board. Otherwise he would leave and go back to his career in pharmacy.

The brothers agreed, but never really stopped meddling in the affairs of the company. Within a few months, it was decided that the only path toward peace was to break up the company into three separate holdings. So the hard work and example of the first Richard Owens came to a swift and inglorious end at the hands of his sons. Lesson: Family business is a lot more complicated than it looks.

Rules of the road for families in business

- Structures: Family businesses change fundamentally over time: from founder/dominant owner–manager to siblings to cousins. Each of these stages has distinct needs and requires different structures. Families must be aware of this.
- Process: Founders and families need to think more in terms of process than in terms of result. When more family members become involved in changing structures, a process is the solution. It must be open, honest and flexible.
- Rules: No individual is bigger than the family, the business and the family business. It is important to establish rules early on.
- Culture/DNA: The importance and impact of the family business history, starting with the founder, cannot be overestimated. The history is the key to future success for families in business.

4
Successful Transitions: Essential Questions and Some Role Models

> A great family makes a great company, a great company makes a great family.
>
> —Gildo Zegna, fourth generation

Thought and planning lie at the heart of successful generational transitions. Before jumping headlong into action, each new generation is well advised to ask the following three fundamental questions – as individuals and as a family – to clarify strategy and avoid problems down the road:

1. Who are we?
   Our DNA: values, principles, competences and culture
2. What do we want?
   Our ownership vision: growth strategies
3. How will we decide?
   Governance structures for family and business.

In the present chapter we will examine these questions in greater detail and look at how some successful family businesses answered them – albeit not without encountering some stumbling blocks on the way. The key idea we want to emphasize is that, throughout generations, many successful multi-generational family businesses seem to follow a logical strategic evolution, which derives from a strong sense of identity. It is this identity that provides roots, reference points and benchmarks, as well as the ability to adapt to changing markets and environments. The answer to the question: "Who

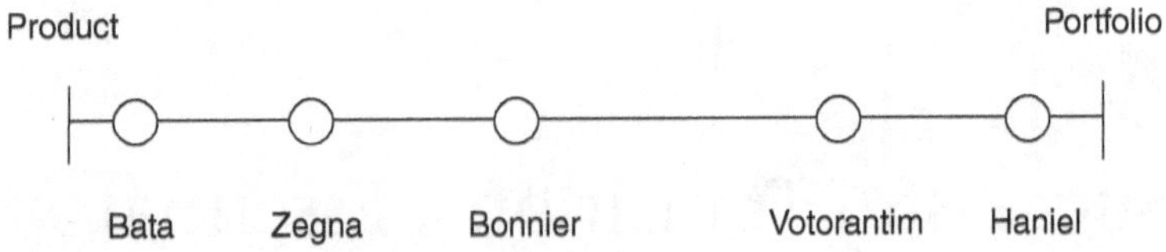

Figure 4.1 Family culture reflects strategy

are we as a family in business?" reflects the family's DNA (taken in a real, non-metaphorical sense) and influences the firm's strategy, which can be positioned on a spectrum at any point between pure product orientation and portfolio approach (see Figure 4.1). In our examples, Bata, the third-generation shoe manufacturer, has consistently focused on shoes as a core product throughout its history, first in manufacturing and then in expanding into retail. At the other end of the scale, the more than 250-year-old German conglomerate Haniel is involved in industries as diverse as pharmaceuticals and healthcare, textiles, raw materials trading and recycling for the steel industry, and mail order business equipment.

A proactive approach by each generation, individually and collectively, to building a shared understanding of "who we are" is the foundation for the second explicitly addressed question, "What do we want?." Exploring the answers allows the family to define its vision, which will have an impact on its growth strategies. Finally, the third question, "How do we decide?," relates to governance structures, which become increasingly important as the family grows.

Generational question 1: Who are we?

This question requires a thorough analysis of the company's history. The members of each new generation must truly understand how and why the business was started, and they can do this by interviewing elders and stakeholders and by hearing their stories. Only after gaining an appreciation and understanding of the past can one make a link with the family's values today and with what they mean in the present. Families should embark on this journey of discovery together.

Many years of accompanying next-generation members through a generational transition have convinced us of the benefits of creating an explicit process whereby the new generation finds its connection to the past. Explaining the evolution of the business, from the founding generation to the present, through charts and numbers is one way of doing it; but it is vital to bring meaning to this evolution. We have found that storytelling by elders, family or not, is one of the most compelling drivers for motivating the next generation to decide on a role of responsible and committed ownership and, possibly, management.

One of the most compelling stories was told by Sam Johnson – fourth-generation leader of the U.S.-based S.C. Johnson Family Enterprises – about how his father, going through a tough business period, returned invigorated after a daring trip to Brazil. Herbert Fisk Johnson Jr. bought an amphibious plane in 1935 and led a 22,000-mile expedition to the heart of Brazil, to study the Carnauba palm tree, which provided the main ingredient for the Johnson family's wax business. He left a book to his son, in which he noted: "Sammy, I hope you take this trip someday. It changed my life. Love, Dad." In 1998, having reconstructed an exact copy of his father's plane, Sam took his two sons on the same trip his father had embarked on over 60 years earlier.

Answering the question "Who are we?" involves an amalgam of different components: discovering shared history and values, understanding accepted principles and the glue that holds the family and the business together. The families that are more successful in business take a careful, enlightened and structured approach to helping the next generation with this task. Finding an answer to this question will help members of the younger generation with their own decisions on which direction to take for *their* future. A meaningful past can provide a more meaningful future, as the example of the Zegna Group shows.

Ermenegildo Zegna Group: Alignment of family values over four generations

Angelo Zegna, founder of the Ermenegildo Zegna Group, was born in 1859 in Italy. By the time he was 40, he operated a textile manufacturing plant. When the factory was destroyed by fire, he rebuilt it in

1907 in the small town of Trivero. Of his ten children, his youngest son, Ermenegildo, quickly emerged as the next leader of the family business, which would eventually become one of the largest and most dynamic in Italy.

Having worked closely with his father, Ermenegildo understood the business well. But he had a very different concept of what it meant to be an entrepreneur. He believed in a more humane approach to leadership and was convinced that technological advances would be the key to the future.

In 1930 Zegna began producing high-quality textiles using machines imported from England. The name Zegna soon became synonymous with fine fabrics. In 1942, the company was split into Ermenegildo Zegna and Sons and a new establishment under the control of Ermenegildo's brother Mario.

The business continued to flourish, as workers were motivated to work for a company with a conscience. After World War II, Ermenegildo, in close cooperation with his sons Angelo and Aldo, concentrated on modernizing the company's manufacturing plants. The focus of attention gradually shifted to the creation of new designs and styles, although manufacturing remained at the heart of everything the company did. As suits became increasingly common in the workplace after the war, and as tailors – the company's traditional clients – gradually declined in number, Zegna decided to expand its activities to include the production of ready-made suits on a large scale.

Convinced of their successful business model as a producer of both fabrics and suits in Italy, the brothers started to look to expansion and risk diversification. They launched their first foreign plant for ready-made suits in 1973. Meanwhile, growing demand had created production bottlenecks, which were exacerbated by an increasingly unstable labor situation. It became ever more difficult to work and plan in this unpredictable economic environment. Then Zegna looked at the Italian part of Switzerland as a production location that would help them avoid some of these difficulties. Building on their expertise in ready-to-wear men's suits, they now also offered made-to-measure suits at a reasonable cost, which was made possible by the rise of computer-aided design and manufacturing techniques.

The brothers became entrepreneurs in their own right and took the family business to new heights, but always with an eye to tradition.

Ownership was shared equally. Meanwhile, the fourth generation of the Zegna was growing up. As their father had done, Angelo and Aldo brought up their children with an open mind, encouraging them to travel, study abroad and learn languages, yet always remembering the family's Italian roots. Their two sons – Gildo and Paolo, respectively – emerged as natural leaders. Before joining the family business and working their way up the ranks, they broadened their horizons by working for other companies in different countries.

The business continued to grow through the opening of new markets and plants. The range of products included suits, ties, knitwear, shirts, accessories, sportswear and the traditional line of fine fabrics. But the company expanded further and entered the retail side of the business, in an effort to get even closer to the client and convey its vision of quality. In 1980, Zegna opened its first retail store in Paris. Dozens of retail stores followed around the world, but they had a strict profit orientation. If breakeven was not achieved within three years, the stores were closed.

In 1998 Gildo and Paolo became joint CEOs, coinciding with the launch of a comprehensive strategy of vertical integration, diversification and brand extension, which included the creation of men's fragrances and accessories. The company's dynamic growth strategy is evident in its Zegna Sport sportswear line, its entry into the women's clothing market and its joint ventures or long-term agreements with Salvatore Ferragamo, stylist Tom Ford and Perofil (among others).

The business is still firmly in the hands of the fourth generation and ownership remains equally divided between the two branches of family. Family control is assured through restrictions on share sales – a family member can sell shares only to another family member, and only at a stipulated and discounted price. Family ties appear strong, allowing strides to be made in financial transparency in order to provide responsible and open reporting to the board and owners.

Zegna is an example of a successful business built on tradition and the values of respect, trust, hard work, excellence and creativity. By maintaining what their ancestors had built, members of each generation indicated respect for the achievements of the past; by adding another step in the value chain with each succeeding generation of the Zegna, they helped foster a real appreciation for and belief in entrepreneurship as an imperative. It is this combination of respect for the past and entrepreneurial freedom for each new generation that makes the Zegna Group a compelling example and role model for multi-generational family businesses. Evolutionary change can provide a more sustainable approach over generations, in contrast to more abrupt revolutionary changes made by new generations. Today, still, the family's guiding principles reflect the perseverance, dedication, intelligence and vision of the founder a century ago.

Generational question 2: What do we want?

The answer to this question is: both clarity and vision. Often the first generation, the entrepreneur, creates clarity and vision during the firm's development. Trial and error gradually lead, by a process of elimination, to a vision of what is desirable and feasible. When companies are successful, the vision for the future is generally robust, based on hard work and tested under difficult conditions. The entrepreneur feels entitled to insist that the next generation adopts this vision and makes it its own. But, while the entrepreneur's vision is the outcome of a singular, sustained effort, members of the next generation may not feel a connection to the business in the same way. Lacking the experience of hard-won success, they need to go through the process of constructing their own vision. This is what is called "buy-in." The commitment of the next generation to ownership, and possibly management, is never greater than when it is the result of a well-considered, deliberate effort. We have seen many senior generations questioning this: "Why leave so much up to the next generation? They might come up with fancy new ideas." This fear can be addressed by giving the senior generation a voice in the approval of the next generation's vision.

Each generation needs to construct its own vision explicitly. That is, members must align their interests and determine what they want to achieve as owners – individually and collectively – and as a generation making a mark on the family and business. An example of a broad-based vision statement created by a next generation group is shown in the box below. The process of developing this statement provided the family members with a better understanding of one another and with the opportunity to construct together a shared vision. One key element in their success was the ability to accept diversity among family members, and even to see differences as a source of strength.

Family business vision statement

- Our family's enduring goal is to ensure harmony, goodwill and compassion within the family, while growing and keeping safe a business that we can pass on, so as to benefit succeeding generations.
- We respect the vision and values of our founders.
- We are proud of our family and its heritage and we strive to capture the enthusiasm and commitment during each generation of family ownership.
- We recognize that unity is our family's strength and that it can only be achieved through excellent communication, love and a respect for one another's differences.
- We shall strive to do what is the right thing for the business in the long term, even though it sometimes may mean short-term sacrifice.
- We are committed to running our business on the basis of sound business principles, for the long-term benefit of the family.

Growing families, in particular, will find the process of jointly thinking about and formulating a future approach helpful in achieving clarity on multiple levels. This clarity also needs to be communicated to the broader range of stakeholders, for instance employees, the community and suppliers. One fundamental aspect next-generation family members need to consider is the issue of staying together as a growing family. Looking at Figure 4.2, we can see the exponential growth in the number of family members from past to present and also anticipate growth in the family in the future. This gives rise to one question: Can the current business accommodate the ownership needs of a family increasing in size? The larger the number of family owners, the more passive and financially oriented they tend to become. Hence there is a need for financial risk diversification inside the family ownership structure, in order to avoid exits by individual members (for personal ownership risk diversification),which would weaken the shared capital base.

An example of a business that dealt with this question extremely well is the German Haniel family, owner of the Haniel Group. The

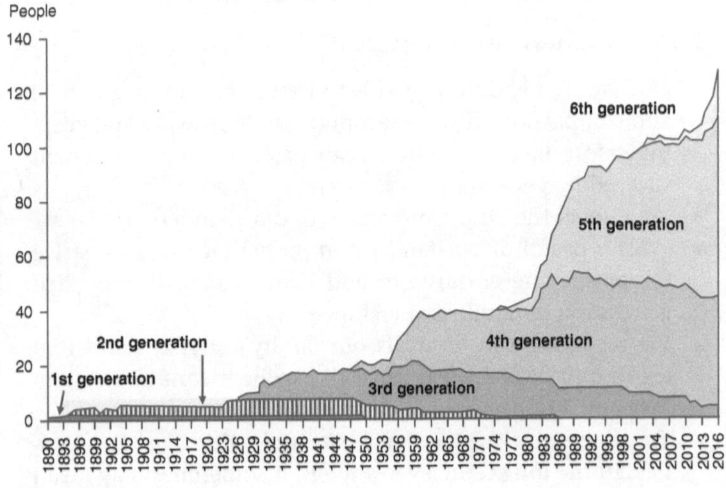

Figure 4.2 Plotting family growth

company was founded more than 250 years ago and today counts well over 560 family shareholders. They made a strategic decision to replace an older, mature business with a group of faster-growing, unrelated businesses. The original businesses today generate only a fraction of annual revenues (see Figure 4.3).

A family of this size requires a business strategy that is built on growth, transparency, professionalism and risk diversification. Their commitment and history as long-term owners provide strong value added to the various business units, which are run by non-family managers.

As Figure 4.4 shows, growth in the business must keep pace with – or preferably even be ahead of – expansion in the family, if the family wants to stay together in the long run. If the family curve continues to go up, the ownership strategy must take this trend into account. Failure to do so can push disaffected owners to seek an exit, as the dividends and ability to influence the company decline. The business may suffer from a lack of engaged and committed ownership.

Both Votorantim Group and the Bata Shoe Organization are examples of family businesses that have adjusted their visions and strategies to take account of generational expansion, even if they have not reached anywhere near the number of shareholders of Haniel – yet!

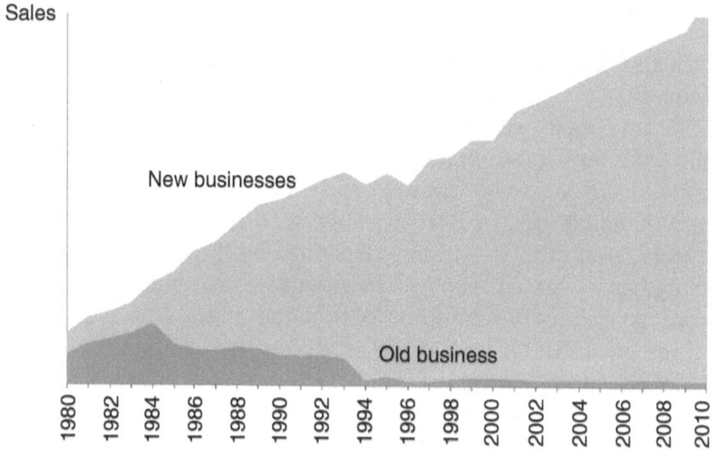

Figure 4.3 Haniel: A business growth vision
Source: Derived from company information.

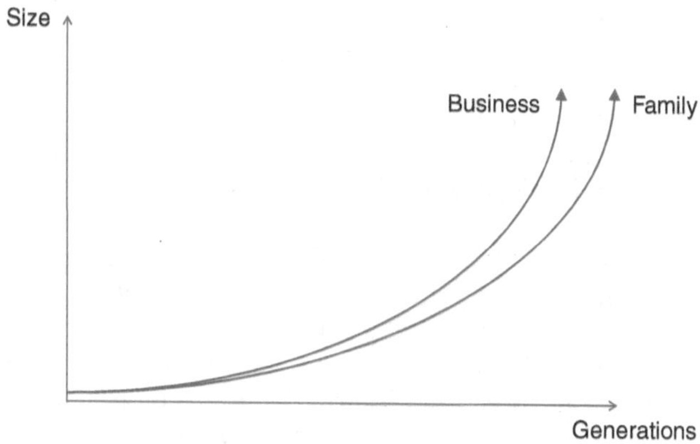

Figure 4.4 The growth curves

Votorantim Group: A passion for Brazil and a shared vision for the future of the business

Brazil's Votorantim Group is a third-generation family business and one of Latin America's largest companies, with a widely diversified portfolio of businesses including cement, steel, aluminum, paper and pulp, energy, finance and orange juice. It operates mainly throughout

Brazil and in fourteen other countries, including the U.S., France and Germany.

The firm began with Antonio Pereira Ignacio, who emigrated as a child from Portugal to Brazil in 1884. Although he started his career there as a shoemaker, he came to believe that there was a huge opportunity in edible oils. In 1905 he established the Fábrica de Oléos de Santa Helena. In 1918 Antonio expanded by buying a small textile factory headed for bankruptcy. The enterprise was renamed Sociedade Anonyma Fabrica Votorantim. Within five years, Votorantim had become one of the largest textile producers in São Paulo. Through a chance encounter with José Ermírio de Moraes, a member of a prominent business family in Brazil, Ignacio became convinced that, in the future, cement and metals would be more profitable.

José and Antonio took the small textile firm to new heights. However, the Great Depression soon wiped out U.S. demand for its products. But the two men found inspiration in their shared vision. They believed Brazil had a promising future and that significant investment in infrastructure would soon be undertaken.

Throughout the 1930s and 1940s, Votorantim's strategy extended to entering basic industries like cement, steel and chemicals. In 1948 the firm created Votocel, in order to develop its presence in paper and pulp. By the 1950s, the group began refining sugar and producing aluminum and hydroelectric power. Following Antonio's death in 1951 José became president, and the second generation of family joined the company. Votorantim's growth was limited through lack of access to the newest technologies. The firm borrowed heavily to finance the licensing of smelter technology, but things did not work out as planned at the new plant and the company struggled to pay down the debt incurred in order to finance this project. It was not until the mid-1960s that the group finally achieved a semblance of financial stability. The painful memories associated with the heavy debt load left an indelible mark on the firm's psyche – a lesson that has stayed with the family ever since.

In the 1980s, the third generation of family managers arrived. They began a strategy of both related and unrelated diversification, by expanding into new lines of business as well as into other regions of Brazil. In the early 1990s the group opened Banco Votorantim. At the same time, Brazil introduced major market reforms, which significantly reduced import tariffs. Suddenly Votorantim had to compete with the best producers in the world. Family members had some painful decisions to make. The group shed many operations in which it was no longer competitive – businesses to which the family had an emotional connection.

Historically, the Votorantim Group had been structured around independent business units, each of which was run by a different family member. The owner/manager philosophy had served the family business well over the first two generations; when José transferred control of the business to his three sons and one son-in-law in 1960, each was responsible for a separate business unit. However, it became apparent that, with the transition to the larger cousin generation, a new governance structure would be needed. The third generation assumed the task of managing a smooth succession.

Aware that few family businesses successfully make such a transition, the leaders of the firm and family decided to tackle the issue head-on. They crafted a two-pronged governance structure, with one board for family and one for business. The family board would seek to incorporate the family's values and ensure transparency in the company. The business board would be tasked with enhancing shareholder value. Through this action, in 2001, the twenty-three members of Votorantim's third generation broke from eight decades of tradition. In total, thirteen cousins working in the group removed themselves from management positions, which were assumed by non-family managers.

The family concluded that, with over fifty members in the fourth generation, it had become too large to rely on informal methods for developing leaders and building family cohesion. Today there are over thirty family shareholders, and the business strategies are largely centered on unrelated business diversification, a situation that reflects the ownership risk diversification of a growing family in business. But the family's core values are always at the heart of any decisions, which they have leveraged to reinvent themselves to ensure the ongoing success of both family and business.

Bata Shoe Organization: The courage to stand up for family principles

Tomas Bata founded the Bata Shoe Organization in what was then Czechoslovakia in 1894. For its first forty years or so it went from strength to strength and took an innovative approach to conducting business, slashing shoe prices by half after currency devaluations in the wake of World War I; introducing profit sharing in 1923; and encouraging every employee to be an entrepreneur. To get around the introduction of customs tariffs in 1931, the company set up factories in other European countries and in the U.S. and India.

When Tomas died in a plane crash in 1932, Thomas Bata Sr. inherited the company from his father. But, since he was only 17, he was not yet ready to operate the global enterprise on his own. A handwritten memo apparently selling the business to Tomas's half-brother Jan meant that Jan began running the business. A "moral testament" was discovered after Tomas's death; it served as the philosophical basis for the firm's operations, which far surpassed the pursuit of money. The firm was to provide a means to improve life in the communities in which it operated. An equally important goal was to give customers the possibility to purchase products of good value.

By the time World War II broke out, the company was producing 60 million pairs of shoes a year in more than thirty countries. At the end of the war, all of the company's assets in Eastern Europe were nationalized and the family fled to safety in Canada, where Thomas Bata Sr. began playing a more active role in management. Subsequently, when he felt he was ready to run the company alone, there was a period of uncertainty.

It was not until 1966, when court battles ended, that Bata Sr. became the clear owner of the company. Deeply affected by this struggle for ownership and by the instability the company suffered as a result, Bata Sr. established two Bermuda trusts to hold the 80 percent of shares not controlled by a charitable foundation.

In 1984, Thomas Bata Jr. (Tom) became the CEO of the firm and his father, Thomas Sr., retired and joined the newly created supervisory board. Two trustees controlling the Bermuda trusts also assumed seats on the board, along with several outside directors. Friction developed when Tom initiated changes to raise the profitability of the company and, therefore, the dividends paid to the family by the trust. Tom became frustrated when the actions designed to improve the firm's performance were received coldly by the board. He had already made a difficult decision – moving operations from Bata's home country of Canada to cheaper production locations in Asia. His next suggestion was a partial listing on an Asian stock exchange, designed to raise much needed capital. The board said "no" to this. Tom felt he could not get the cooperation he needed, so he resigned as CEO in 1993.

The major impediment that Tom saw to the company's future was its strange ownership structure. Trustees who held the sole power to appoint their successors were in charge of his birthright. But, given the fact that his name was on the door, he felt he cared more about the company than the trustees did. So, in 2001, after more years of dire company performance, Tom convened a meeting with his three sisters. They could no longer stand by and watch the family firm decline. They presented a united front to their parents, the trustees and the board members. They wanted their company back and they were willing to go to court to get it. To their surprise, their proposal was greeted positively and, after some more court machinations, they ended up being in control of the company.

In 2002, to reinvent its core competencies, Bata opened innovation centers around the world, to develop shoes with exclusive comfort features and designs; this was followed by the launch, in 2009, of the European Shoe Innovation Center in Padua, Italy. In a further illustration of its values, the company is nearing the completion of a 262-acre riverside estate designed to modernize its factory in Kolkata through 2,500 homes for employees, a school and hospital. The third generation knows what it wants and has restructured and adapted the company to changing markets in order to pursue its dream.

Generational question 3: How will we decide?

The third important question for the next generation involves governance. Comprehensive governance structures are particularly important at a time of generational transition. When it comes to who decides what, clarity throughout the entire process is needed. We often think about the creation of governance structures in families as a process of creating democracy. The rules of the game are the same: honesty, fairness, transparency, equality and shared objectives. To this must be added rules, guidelines for behavior, and broadly accepted criteria that allow decisions to be made in the interests of all.

Following the logic of the three-circle model over time (as discussed in Chapter 3), once a growing family business is past the founder and owner/manager stage, it is imperative for it to separate conceptually the three levels of family, ownership and business. Family needs to find a way to communicate and make decisions about relevant issues. A family council can be created, to formalize this process and to delegate tasks to a smaller body or to committees. The main task of the family council is to launch the development of a family constitution. This document should be the basis for "operationalizing" the vision statement.

At the ownership level, an owners' council evaluates and guides investment in the family firm, as well as other investments in the family's portfolio, from an owner's point of view. This perspective is different to that of a business board. The ownership aspect has to consider the overall wealth of the family. It is about risk diversification, which typically involves assessment of unrelated investments and business diversification strategies. As such, resource allocations are decided at the highest possible level.

At the business level, the board of directors supervises and steers the company's activities. This approach is different from the ownership perspective, since it tends to emphasize the value extracted from a particular business.

It is also possible to take a two-pillared approach to governance structures. Earlier, also in Chapter 3, we mentioned that families in business are confronted with the complexities caused by the overlap of two different systems: family (the "socialist" system) and business (the "capitalist" system). The two-pillared governance structure allows for the logical and effective separation and integration of the different systems. On the ownership side, decisions are made according to relative ownership among family members, using a business board with independent non-family directors. The underlying principles are performance and competence.

On the family side, decisions are made equally: one family member, one vote. Addressing the needs of a diverse group of family members is the primary concern. The family as a community takes center stage. Institutionalized support structures are created for those who need them: educational stipends, emergency funds for families in need, fiscal and other advisory services. In addition, philanthropic activities are enabled and coordinated.

An example of excellence in the creation of a durable, viable governance structure is the Swedish Bonnier Group.

Bonnier Group: Re-examining governance structures every generation

The Bonnier Group is the largest publishing and media company in Scandinavia, comprised of over 175 individual entities. The current

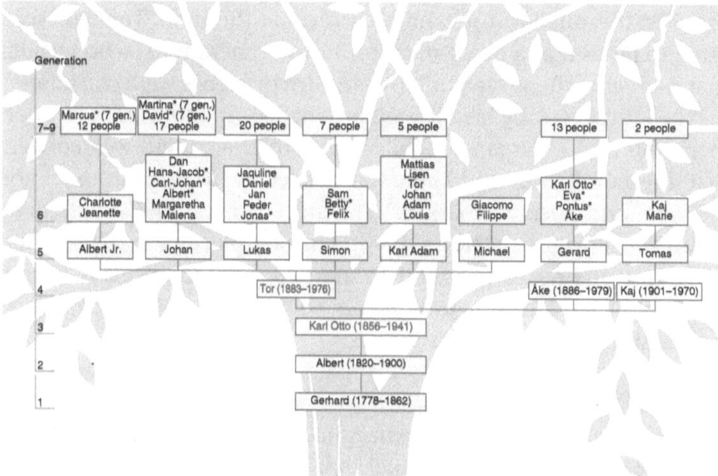

Figure 4.5 Bonnier: 9 generations, 76 owners
*Working in the family business.
Source: Hans-Jacob Bonnier, "A History of Transfers of Ownership." Presentation, Stockholm, March 2010.

ownership is in the hands of more than seventy family members from three generations (the fourth, the fifth and the sixth) and moving into the seventh (see Figure 4.5). The founder was born in Germany in 1778 and, in his early twenties, moved to Denmark. Making a fresh start in a new land, he started a book store. His eleven children followed in his footsteps. They started newspapers and magazines and launched publishing companies throughout Sweden.

It was central to the family and business culture to develop deep and lasting relationships with authors. As a result of this early exposure to literature, the family's children were intellectually curious and gained an education beyond their years. The boundaries between family and commerce receded and the family became closely identified with its media business.

After three generations of ownership concentrated in a single man, control of the company came to be shared, though not evenly. The fourth generation pursued a more aggressive expansionist business model, emphasizing magazine publishing through acquisition. This represented a significant risk, as the price of the acquired company equalled the value of the family business at the time. The deal soon came to be seen as a benchmark for future generations, who recalled that moment whenever similarly large investments were considered.

The Bonnier family business maintained a strong position in book, magazine and newspaper publishing. However, there was concern that the family was still too concentrated on the communication industry and specific markets. The fifth generation launched an expansion into unrelated fields, which took place over thirty years, right until the death of Albert Jr. in 1989. The group made investments in paper, furniture production, packaging, engineering, a ferry service and other diverse businesses.

As time passed, some family members asked to be bought out, and shares were redistributed. From three owners in the fourth generation, the number of family owners had grown to seven in the fifth generation; but they had unequal shareholdings. For the business to gain clarity and cohesion, a fifty-year ownership contract was signed that stated the family's desire to stay united, build the business and sell shares only to other family members.

Succession from the fifth to the sixth generation represented a paradigm shift for the family and for the business. Up to the fifth generation, the dominant owner concept had prevailed – even though the number of owners had grown. In the early 1990s, the sixth generation, with almost thirty members, was coming on the scene as the family expanded, and the fifth generation gave them the opportunity to create their own vision. The process and the outcome were powerful. The vision indicated a stronger focus on the family's publishing roots, away from unrelated diversification, as well as the creation of a base for broader involvement of family members in ownership: for the first time, women could hold shares and work in the business. And, most importantly, the process laid the groundwork to enable members of each generation to decide by themselves and for themselves their ownership vision. In fact, the validity of a new generation's shareholder agreement was reduced from fifty years to thirty years. It will be up to the next generation to decide on its vision.

The new governance structure, with seventy-six family owners in 2010, separates business from family matters (see Figure 4.6). The company, refocused on a media strategy, is controlled by a holding company in which family members explicitly define their ownership

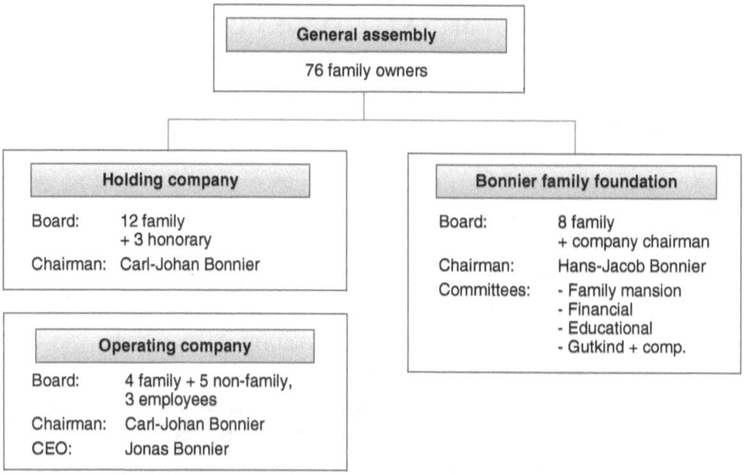

Figure 4.6 Bonnier Group governance structures 2010
Source: Joachim Schwass (from company information).

approach. These decisions flow into the business through the board of directors of the operating company, with five family members, five non-family members and three employee members. For family matters such as social and educational issues, a family foundation was created and is run by a different set of family members from the one that oversees the business.

Another turning point came in 1998, when the Bonnier family had a major decision to make: either to merge the Bonnier Group into a publicly traded publishing company in which it had a stake, thus providing access to public capital and an exit opportunity for family; or to buy and merge this entity into the Bonnier Group. The Bonnier cousins chose the second option. The emotional attachment to the media industry was so strong that the family was willing to pay the substantial price of this acquisition. Several times, in earlier generations, the Bonniers had proven their willingness to accept large risks for the sake of the company's future. Now they did it again.

Over the years, the Bonnier family has demonstrated the ability both to identify opportunity and to rethink its approach to family *and* business when it was necessary. The Bonnier's flexibility in responding to changes in family and business while retaining a keen devotion to the core business and to family ethos will probably hold the group in good stead for generations to come.

The secrets of success

In essence, generational transition implies a period of change and upheaval. Families need to consider how to avoid the predictable traps when they move from one business and family culture to another. As we have seen, in particular in the examples of Haniel Group, Votorantim Group and Bonnier Group, a growing family requires a growing business. This brings along its own pressures and possibilities. Larger families may have too many cooks spoiling the broth. What is the best way to divide shares fairly? How can control be sufficiently concentrated for the company to stay in the family, yet not so centered as to exclude most of its members? Providing exit opportunities for family members who will inevitably lack either the interest or the ability to act as responsible owners is a crucial challenge. The ultimate test may be to try to keep the family together in spite of everything – size, possible lack of engagement of some members with the business, and all the other hurdles that may beset a large ownership group.

Clarity is required, and it should come through an open process, which encourages asking three key questions, along with a willingness to identify the answers collectively:

1. Who are we? – How do we honor our history, leverage the power of our values and acknowledge and sustain the DNA – the glue – that holds us together?
2. What do we want? – A lack of alignment of interests among stakeholders will almost certainly doom a family in business. The only way to stay together as a family and company is to come to a consensus on purpose, goals and objectives.
3. How will we decide? – Governance structures and vehicles that instill transparency and clarity are simple, yet critical to success, cohesion and happiness as a family. As in many other realms within a family business, the process seems to be the most important part of the equation. You will not be able to think of and provide for every possible situation you may face over the next twenty years. But designing a system that makes sense and gains

agreement from all on a philosophical approach to problem-solving is a big step forward in helping keep family and the business on the right track.

Rules of the road for families in transition

- Structures: Establishing transparent governance bodies for family and the business is crucial at every stage. It gets more complicated as the family grows and generational transitions take place. Consensus must be gained that promotes a happy, cohesive family, which supports its business.
- Process: Family councils, family constitutions and shareholder agreements can all contribute to healthy family relationships. The next generation must be free to craft its own way forward – structures, agreements, succession plans and financial arrangements. If the older generation tries to impose its own will on these questions, discord frequently results. The most important thing is for all participants to feel they have options and a voice.
- Rules: Take care to define family broadly, in the context of family governance, and to keep as many as possible actively engaged, according to their skills and abilities. Trouble often arises when people feel trapped or unheard. The family's role in, and relationship with, the business should be clearly defined. The company must have a robust board, including family members, and several strong and respected independent directors.
- Culture/DNA: The source of a family firm's unanimity lies in family values, as started by the firm's founder and kept tangible and real by the family leaders and by the dedicated employees who followed them. It is important for families in business to sustain the DNA – the glue – that holds them together.

5
The Future – The Family Office

The only question with wealth is what you do with it...
—Attributed to John D. Rockefeller, Jr.

Given the complexity in strategy, governance and relationships involved in family business, one might marvel that a family ever emerges on the other side and wants to find a permanent way to continue together. But many families that have successfully accumulated significant wealth begin to search for a means to preserve it for present and future generations. One way to do so is to form a family office. Although definitions differ, a family office is generally organized to manage and leverage the family's collective wealth, with an emphasis on stewardship rather than growth. Stewardship implies a long-term view and looks at inherited wealth as something to be treasured and preserved, in real terms, for future generations of family. A sense of stewardship is a powerful motivator, in the first place, not to destroy the financial and philosophical legacy of the founder and, second and ideally, to extend the reach of these resources into the modern day.

We are going to talk extensively about the family office, as it is a model for how to manage family wealth. But we have also found that many professional people and budding entrepreneurs can benefit from the logic and insights presented in connection with the family office. In the life cycle of successful family businesses, the liquidity generated, over the years, from excess cash flows or from the sale of the company can call for a different approach. For the founder, the passion, the entrepreneurship, the successful guiding of the family company through rough times and the desire to control the whole process may be challenged. Above all, managing excess cash may be not as interesting as managing the company. This is where the family office comes in.

The institution known as a family office started over a century ago, but it has evolved and changed over the years. Each family office is different, since this institution reflects the core values and needs of individual families. Some family offices focus mainly on preserving and growing the financial assets; others are primarily a forum for philanthropy. However, family cohesion is most often their overarching aim and, with any luck, their outcome. The first family offices were founded by entrepreneurs responsible for two of the world's earliest mega-fortunes. Thomas Mellon, who amassed the Pittsburgh-based Mellon Bank fortune, started the first family office in 1868. John D. Rockefeller followed closely afterwards, in the late 1880s, with his own family office, which was intended to concentrate the wealth he had earned operating Standard Oil. In 1913 he set up the Rockefeller Foundation, in an effort to focus the substantial charitable donations he was already making to religious, educational and social welfare causes.

One of the chief roles of a family office is to keep a close eye on the family's investment portfolio, often by hiring its own managers instead of entrusting the funds to a financial institution. In this way the family may be better able to accomplish both its financial goals and its ambitions of living in harmony with the founder's philosophy. Keeping the family intact as it expands numerically, and perhaps geographically, has become another important objective. By pooling funds and making the family office the center of family governance and collective action, many families reason that they stand a better chance of staying united and true to their family values while maintaining confidentiality and privacy.

As the family grows, the complexity of the governance increases. The following three examples show a family over four generations with different growth scenarios, which all present potential problems. In Figure 5.1, the family is growing faster than the investment/family business. Even though most of the family remains in the home country, complexity increases quickly and the family will find itself in difficulty, as the pie is too small to share among the increasing number of members.

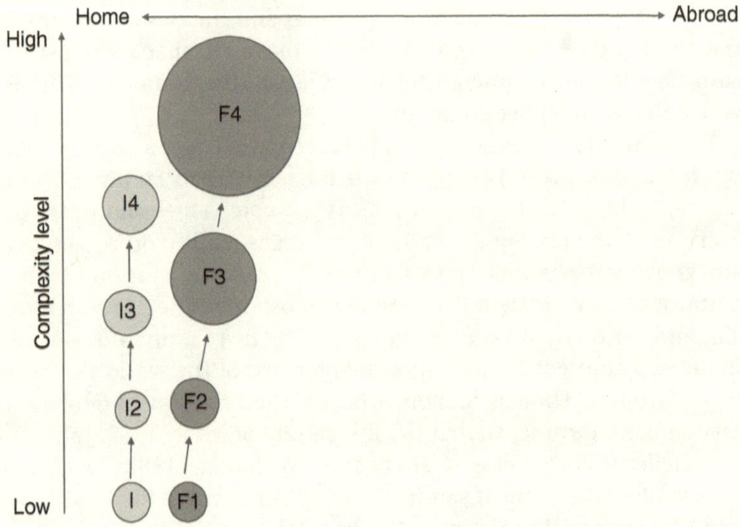

Figure 5.1 Family governance complexity: Fast-growing family

Rapid expansion abroad is not necessarily the answer, as Figure 5.2 illustrates. In this case, the family stays small and mainly in the home country, but the investment/family business becomes larger and very international. This can present problems, as there are not enough family members on the ground to support this rapid global expansion.

When the family becomes more scattered – living, say, in five or six countries on two or three continents – but the business remains rooted in the country of origin, many family members become passive investors, losing their connection to the business and to the home country (see Figure 5.3).

If the family and the business grow at similar speeds, it is easier to embrace the growing complexities of family governance. Figure 5.4 illustrates this process in a home country setting; and, even though only a minority of family members is active in the firm, communication with the rest of the family remains healthy. In Figure 5.5, parallel growth in investments and the family, even internationally, helps overcome the complexity; this is aided by having both active and passive family members close to the investments/family business.

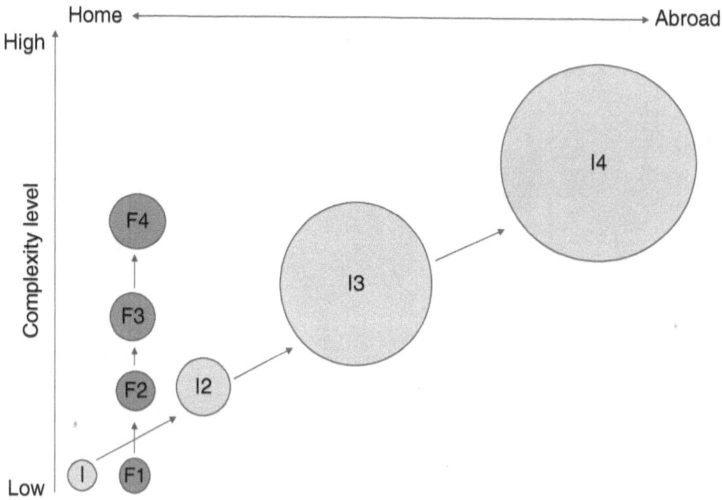

Figure 5.2 Family governance complexity: International expansion of the business

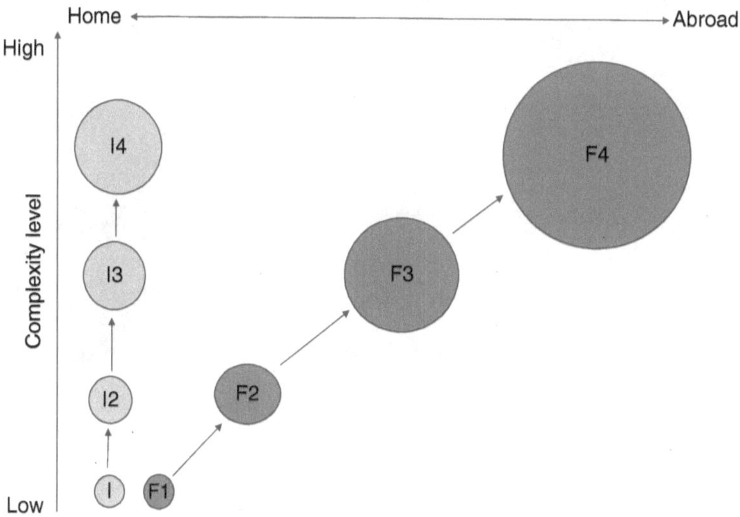

Figure 5.3 Family governance complexity: Local investment, global family

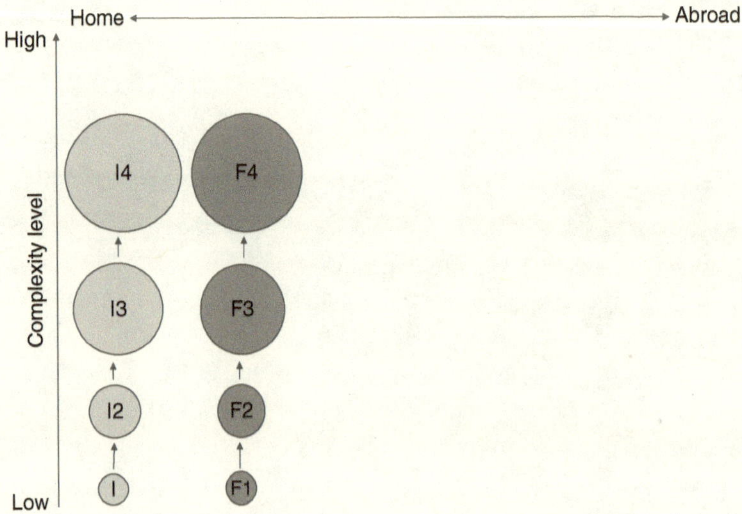

Figure 5.4 Family governance complexity: Parallel growth at home

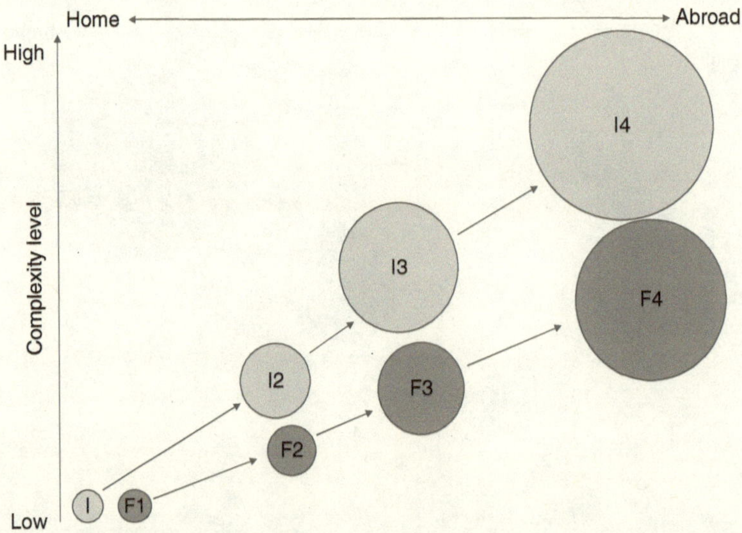

Figure 5.5 Family governance complexity: Parallel growth abroad

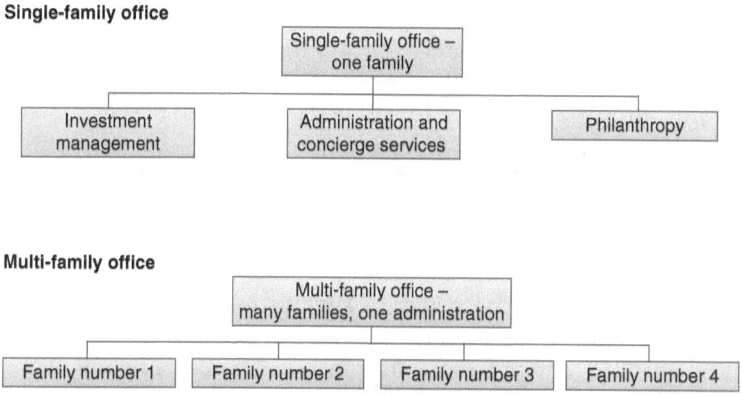

Figure 5.6 Single-family office vs. Multi-family office

How the family grows in concert with its assets has a significant impact on the future of both.

There are two main types of family offices: a single-family office (SFO) and a multi-family office (MFO) (see Figure 5.6). An SFO is a forum for one family's continuity, unity, investing and philanthropy. It often includes investment management (risk management, selection of managers, monitoring and estate planning), concierge services (bill paying, property and fleet management), administration (accounting, tax and legal) and family philanthropy. (See Appendix C for a full listing of potential family office services.)

An MFO, by contrast, generally arises as a result of the success of one family's SFO in fulfilling its mission. That family has itself experienced the potential benefits – such as capacity utilization, better pricing on investment activities or attracting high-quality professional talent as employees – and invites other families to join it in this venture. There is a single, central administrative function to handle the affairs of the families. Chapter 7 discusses the potential benefits and pitfalls of each organizational type in more detail.

Why family offices are started

A family office can be the brainchild of many different actors. It may be started by the company founder, as a way to keep the family united, its members functioning as business owners and torchbearers of his philosophy. The second generation can see a family office as a forum for keeping wealth and control of the business concentrated in the family. Or a subsequent generation may establish a family office in order to carry out the wise investment of dividends or the proceeds from the sale of the family firm.

Precisely who starts the family office can have an impact not just when the office is launched, but also later in the life of this entity. An entrepreneur might design such an organization to maintain his legacy and keep the family together (and possibly away from his company). An office can be a way to attempt to continue to exercise power beyond the grave. And, if a founder is relatively young and is reluctant to retire, he or she may involve himself or herself in the day-to-day operations of the family office. This could be another way to maintain one's position at the helm of the family.

Second-generation members may form an SFO together, or they may choose to have individual ones. Later-stage families face the size and complexity issues associated with a large corporate enterprise. And it is wise to realize that there is as much chance of losing the wealth as there is of growing it. But Kathryn McCarthy, an independent family office consultant, director of the Rockefeller Trust Company, NA and former president of Marujupu LLC, the Sulzberger family office (*New York Times* controlling family), says:

> The second generation is when the "make or break" decisions generally are confronted. Family members must ask themselves whether they want to spend down the wealth accumulated by the founder or save it for posterity. Responding to these issues is made more complex by the growing distance from the entrepreneur. If key questions are not answered in the affirmative by the second generation, the potential for cohesion, rallying around core values and wealth-building is sort of off the table for family members in the future.[1]

As Ben Oehler, an independent advisor to family offices and former president and CEO of Waycrosse, Inc., the family office of the owners of Cargill Incorporated, notes:

> The risk for successive generations is becoming too money-oriented. The further you get away from the founder, the less the emphasis is on wealth creation. The danger is that consumption can crowd out the natural entrepreneurial tendencies of family

> members. It is essential both for these individual family members and for the continued health and well-being of the family that heirs make tangible contributions to the world and their communities. Otherwise, wealth may actually diminish the person's life, rather than enhance it.[2]

A family office, in whatever form or stage, can enable families to:

- Maintain control of their destiny and privacy and retain a measure of financial confidentiality.
- Preserve wealth in real terms and manage assets wisely. Optimizing the risk profile of the SFO is critical to the family's needs.
- Join forces to increase the family's purchasing power or to reduce costs associated with financial products.
- Facilitate succession transition across generations. The more organized and inclusive this process, the better chance a family has of staying together, particularly for a large group.
- Keep family members, whatever their interests and capabilities, engaged with the family, even if they are not directly involved in the business.
- Facilitate the education of future generations of family.
- Learn how to survive in a world of wealth. A family office can be helpful to a family that has built up its knowledge of success in business. Now, the family and its members need to build competence in managing the fruits of that labor and in passing the wealth and the know-how to the next generation.
- Strive for excellence in philanthropic pursuits.
- Keep family and business matters separate.
- Provide a springboard for future family entrepreneurs.
- Create a platform to pass along not only wealth but also values, philosophy and history to the next generation.

Some statistics on family offices

A recent study of European family offices conducted by IMD and the European Private Equity & Venture Capital Association (EVCA)[3] provides some insights into the world of family office:

- Forty three percent of SFOs in the sample were started as a result of the sale of the family company, 28 percent after a partial sale and 14 percent as a result of the accumulation of wealth.

- They invested most frequently in equities, bonds, private equity, hedge funds and real estate.
- A majority of assets was managed either partly or entirely by the family office.
- Many families consider geographic dispersion of assets to be a prudent diversification strategy.

The minimum amount of assets necessary to launch an effective SFO is generally considered to be about $500 million. At lower levels, the costs simply outweigh the financial benefits. Initial set-up costs for an SFO often reach $2 million. Annual operating expenses can range between 0.4 percent and 0.5 percent of investable assets.[4] Of course, this figure varies according to how the family wants to operate its SFO. Depending on the level of service provided to the family, large global SFOs can spend 0.9–1.2 percent of assets on total operating expenses (which include the cost of asset management). The level of operating costs can be influenced by the caliber of the team the family hires to run the SFO. A top-quality management team can help get the best deals on investment fees, IT costs and travel expenses.

Differing challenges and opportunities are present in large, medium and small SFOs. An SFO with fewer family members usually exhibits efficient decision-making, a higher level of assumed risk and a family more involved in its operations.[5] Because the bond between the family and the SFO is close, the institution has wide latitude in making important decisions on the family's behalf. An SFO with more clients who are family members can operate in a more ambiguous and complex decision-making environment and is generally not nimble – just as one would expect.

Other areas in which size can be influential are oversight and governance. When the number of family-member clients (not necessarily investible assets) increases, monitoring and governance of the family office generally becomes more involved.[6]

How to start a family office

Like most things, the matters of how you start and how much time and effort you devote in the initial stages of a project, such as establishing a family office, can have a major impact on its future. Although action usually feels better than pausing and contemplating the bigger picture, a little thought and planning – a period of one to two years is recommended – can pay dividends in the long run.

Wise counselors advise that there are four major issues to consider before taking tangible steps toward a family office:[7]

1. Think about the family's purpose and goals in the widest terms possible, including the family business, the next generation, wealth and philanthropy.
2. Write a mission statement expressing these goals. Define success and how you will know when you have achieved it.
3. Design a business plan addressing specifics such as legal structure, primary activities, governance systems, revenue and expense expectations and the role of the family.
4. Carefully consider what kind of employees you want to attract and retain and how staffing fits in with the overall business plan.

The flow chart in Figure 5.7 can help structure your thinking before we move on to look at the specifics of establishing an SFO, including factors such as location, size, outsourcing, asset management, governance, benchmarking, non-family managers and staffing.

Location

One of the first decisions a family office founder must make is where the office will be located. There are more considerations involved in this question than might be immediately apparent, and there are certainly some places that are very popular for establishing an SFO (see Table 5.1 for a family office locator matrix). For one thing, the local and national tax environment plays a significant role. As with any major concentration of funds in business or personal investing, assessing the relative arduousness and intricacy of the tax, legal and regulatory environment in potential locations is important. All families in business would, of course, seek to fulfill their obligations to tax authorities and regulators, but minimizing the tax bill is a goal common to all taxpayers. Likewise, some locations may come at a higher financial price but be well worth it for the ease of doing business, the social scene or the sheer quality of life.

A family may choose to locate its SFO in its traditional home town. But, as families grow, they tend to spread across geographic borders,

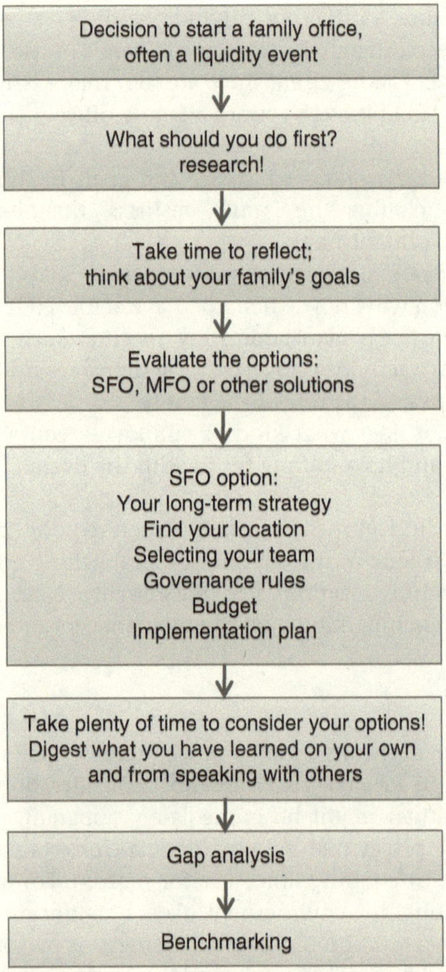

Figure 5.7 Steps to consider when to start an SFO

and even across continents. The decision becomes more complex when family members live around the globe and personally visiting the SFO is not a viable option for all. The location of the family office is also directly influenced by who is setting it up. If it is the founder, he or she may want to be able to drop into the office on a regular basis, so it would need to be located where he or she lives or, anticipating the future, in the city where he or she will retire. If

Table 5.1 Family office locator matrix

	Weighting 5 = Excellent 4 = Good 3 = Satisfactory 2 = Poor 1 = Unsatisfactory	Geneva	Singapore	London	New York	Monaco	Zurich	Bermuda	Hong Kong
1	Tax								
2	Legal								
3	Structure								
4	Access to talented people								
5	Geographic proximity								
6	Banking infrastructure								
7	Personal living/security								
8	School/education								
9	Economic stability								
10	Political stability								
11	Regulation								
12	Professional security/ confidentiality								
13	IT security								
14	Cost								
15	Language								
16	International access								
17	Networking								
18	Climate								
19	Overall risk								
	TOTAL SCORE								

the SFO is established because the family business has been sold or by later generations of family, the decision might simply be based on which locale offers the best tax and legal environment or the most utility for the greatest number of family members.

The legal structure chosen for holding the collective assets can play into this decision, too. Family offices may take the legal form of a corporation or of a trust or some other structure, depending on which jurisdictions offer the optimal structure for the family's needs. Onshore or offshore structures, or a combination of both, could be utilized. The advice of a knowledgeable tax advisor is critical to instituting a structure that fulfills the purpose of the family's SFO while also being user-friendly and flexible. If a location offers a low tax rate, but onerous reporting or other requirements that could compromise privacy, performance or purpose, another city might be a better overall choice.

Security is an issue that may not come immediately to mind as a factor in this important decision. Personal security of family members and the existence of a robust legal infrastructure to protect assets are both major considerations. The question of security is often answered by hiring a specialized firm. With any luck, an SFO is a lasting venture. A thorough understanding of all aspects of the present environment, as well as a sense of the location's longer-term prospects, are absolutely necessary to help avoid disappointment, or even failure.

Size

While to some degree the size of the family office is driven by the cash available for investment, families may not put all their assets into the family office, choosing to place only those funds into the SFO that are required to fulfill its purpose. Cost, family size and service preferences all figure in this calculation. As mentioned earlier in the chapter, $500 million in investible resources is often considered the benchmark size to offset the cost of running an SFO. Although keeping things relatively small might serve the purpose of providing a platform for family cohesion and offers less complication, a larger portfolio would probably allow the family access to more sophisticated asset managers and, therefore, possibly greater financial diversification and potential performance. The economies of scale available to a larger entity could have a beneficial effect on the SFO's bottom line.

Deciding which services the family wants, needs and is willing to pay for is another item family members must agree upon. Concierge and other services, like financial education, which might be seen as extras, will certainly add to the cost of an SFO. But they may also enhance family-member satisfaction and the feeling of belonging to a larger whole, which is at the center of the family office concept.

In-house or outsourced?

Some of the most thorny and complex decisions lie in the realm of which family office operations to retain in-house and which to outsource. There are advantages to each. Although keeping the SFO staff small may lower direct costs and increase flexibility, there are counterpoints to these apparent benefits. Confidentiality, for one, may be sacrificed by outsourcing. The more people have your data, the greater the chances are that your information could be leaked to the wider world. Furthermore, outsourcing can limit professional development opportunities for SFO employees. This may be an enormous impediment in attracting and retaining knowledgeable, capable staff.

Conversely, retaining all SFO functions in-house may cause employees to fall behind the leading edge in innovations in current practice in their specialty and lead to insularity. Outsiders can bring fresh contributions, but they widen the scope of people familiar with the family's circumstances. The right balance between internal and external sourcing must be determined by each family according to its own sensibilities and priorities.

Another factor in considering the degree of outsourcing undertaken by an SFO is of a more technical nature, to do with the systems required to facilitate regular reporting to family members. This is discussed in more detail in Chapter 6.

In general, however, some functions should always be carried out in-house:

- Risk profile of the family/individual family members
- Strategic allocation of assets
- Selection of asset managers
- Risk/portfolio management
- Liquidity management
- Basic legal and tax expertise
- Accounting
- Personal or household services
- Anything else that impacts security, confidentiality or privacy.

Other situations call for an outside influence:

- Having a certain number of non-family, non-executive members helps ensure sound business governance on a family office board.
- Investment committee members, preferably independent and drawn from outside, can bring the advantage of new ideas and

insights into market conditions and can help the family to remain disciplined.
- Niche legal, tax and financing expertise.
- Auditing.

Choosing suitable outsourcing partners is a competency in itself. Trust, reputation, confidentiality and a similar mindset are essential. Asking for advice from other family offices would both ease the difficulty of finding the right service provider and give a sense of current market pricing and terms (see also the section on benchmarking later in this chapter). Hire outside help carefully and with an eye to whether these providers truly understand, and buy into, the family's vision for itself and the role the service provider plays in making it a reality.

Selection of asset managers

Vital to the success of an SFO are the selection of asset managers and the critical evaluation of asset allocation choices. Without a well-designed, flexible portfolio and thoughtful, trustworthy and committed asset managers, the objectives of the family office will be put at risk. The best advice is to approach the selection of asset managers with all the seriousness of choosing a physician. Not only must the individuals performing this vital function for the family be highly intelligent and technically skilled, but they should also have a deep understanding of the softer side of things. A family office, by its nature, is all about the collective aspirations and ambitions of a group of connected people. Asset managers without the proper appreciation of the uniqueness and, dare we say, the sanctity of their mission should be bypassed in favor of more discerning ones. As we all know, however, it is much easier to analyze financial performance than to assess character and motivation accurately. In Chapter 6 we discuss in more detail the crucial issue of portfolio design.

Some families consider it essential that asset management operations be done internally. The main reasons for this are the preference for confidentiality, control and customized products. The family office may also want to maintain these competencies inside the organization in order to develop internal expertise. In addition, not every provider has both the performance track record and the customer service orientation that will satisfy SFOs.

If you do employ external service providers, keep track of their performance. Follow up with regular site visits, telephone calls or video conferences; show that you take an active interest. You should be able to challenge the asset manager on the details of his investment approach, just as you would challenge an employee in your company on work processes. Be sure to meet the team that will serve the SFO on a daily basis, not just the sales people. The leadership of the family and SFO must feel in sync with these professionals and confident about their commitment, diligence and capability. All performance and liquidity related data should be built into the SFO's own sophisticated reporting system, which provides – at least on a monthly basis – the necessary 360-degree overview of your asset allocation, possible liquidity issues and common ground for discussion on changes in your portfolio weightings.

Governance

SFOs must have top-notch governance processes, procedures and structures in order to accomplish their ambitious aims. Ideally, a family contemplating establishing an SFO will already have set up family governance mechanisms such as a family council and a constitution. A family council basically acts as the wider family's representative and organizing body. Family members vote on who will sit on the council and on what terms. A family would also be well advised to have undergone the related, and at times laborious, process of creating a family constitution. Such a document would set out the basic processes and rules for how the family will handle issues and conflicts. It also generally outlines exit opportunities, stock valuations, criteria for family employment in the family business and next-generation education provisions – among other possibilities.

Families who have these basic building blocks in place for working together as a group often choose to establish a family office as a way to leverage the power of their unity, both financially and philosophically. As part of their governance, many large SFOs create a board to direct their activities; in practice, this is less common in smaller family offices. A Merrill Lynch/Campden Research survey quotes an SFO leader as follows:

> The need for more formal structures becomes critical with the third generation, when family members are not as close to the

original wealth creator or as subject to their control and vision as the preceding generation.[8]

Even if there is no family office board, there may be operating committees, for example those governing investments and management, on which family members can sit. Research shows that about a third of the seats on the critical investment committee are held by family members.[9] This makes good sense, after all. It is their money that is at stake, and their blessing to the investment policies undertaken by the SFO empowers the portfolio managers and improves communication. Family office employees maintain a strong presence on these committees as well. Wise SFO leaders get the input of respected business people on their committees; outsiders can constitute up to one third of investment committee membership.[10] Most of the committees meet on a quarterly basis; investment performance is generally communicated to family members monthly.

The linchpin in this whole system is the family office manager (see Figure 5.8). Sometimes this position is occupied by a family member. But the breadth of knowledge and professional experience, in addition to the many innate qualities required, means that in most cases a non-family manager will lead the organization on a daily basis. A more detailed review of this role follows below.

The lower portion of Figure 5.8 depicts the primary functions performed in most SFOs, depending on what outsourcing decisions

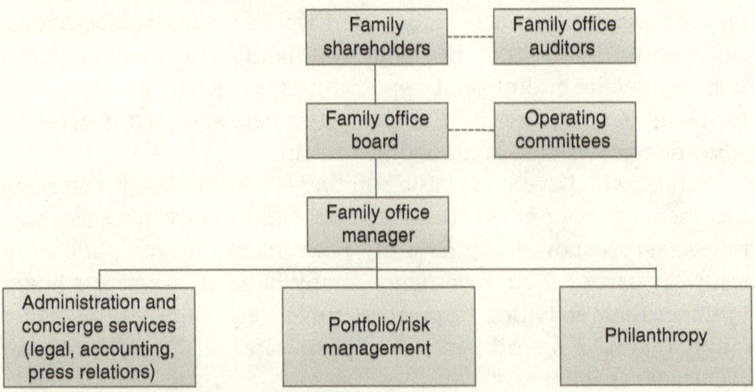

Figure 5.8 Family office structure

have been made. Again, the size and complexity of the SFO often determines what is done and by whom. For example, large SFOs with sizable investible funds at stake routinely have an external audit performed. Many smaller SFOs do not. Enough legal and accounting expertise must be retained inside the organization to make well-reasoned assessments of external providers and to make decisions on the basis of their recommendations.

So far, we have been talking mainly about macro-level issues in the governance of the SFO. However, details are important in keeping the peace among family members and between the SFO and its family clients. To avoid potential conflict, the operating rules for the SFO should be adopted – like the family constitution – before the SFO opens its doors. Important areas on which to gain early family-member agreement include:

- Who participates in the SFO – Family members? (For every family the definition is different – e.g. are in-laws family?) Shareholders?
- What specific services will be offered?
- Who pays for the services and how? – A fee as a percentage of shareholdings? One fee divided by the number of family members? Service user fees? Netted against gains? As with all other processes and decisions of the family office, transparency is essential.
- Who determines the SFO budget, staffing and operating guidelines? (Can it take on debt? What employee benefits/salary will it offer?)
- What are the reporting frequency and committee/governance structures?
- What procedure needs to be followed for a client wishing to exit the family office?

Benchmarking/counsel from other families

The best way to avoid trouble and obtain the most from an SFO is to seek the input of peer institutions. Those who have already founded their own SFO can share what they believe to be best practices. Peer groups can provide a forum for benchmarking and learning from the experiences of others. Most of the good information will come from your informal network. In a pinch, these colleagues will share warnings or positive impressions of service providers. Family offices can learn what the going rate is for services, who the best providers are and what the most pressing issues are in the industry. Just as family businesses operate in an environment in which there are few real peers and therefore they find other family firms to share experiences with, so family offices must search out productive, confidential and reciprocal relationships. But caution is needed here. Since every SFO is unique, it is unlikely that your situation will be exactly the same as that of any other SFO. Take the big-picture advice from peers and then apply your own best judgment.

The role of non-family managers

What is the most important quality for a non-family manager (NFM) of an SFO? The answer is both simple and complex. Simple because trust is the one non-negotiable criterion for a non-family leader of an SFO; complex because a cultural fit with the organization is also essential, but this is less easy to define and gauge.

The NFM runs the day-to-day operations, helps the family strategize about portfolio management, goals and purpose, and is part social worker, part psychologist in working to smooth relationships among family members and between the family and its SFO. He or she needs to be able to straddle the worlds of family, investment management and in-the-trenches leadership. His or her professionalism must be beyond reproach. Yet he or she must also possess an extra something that facilitates a deep understanding of the family's unique goals and motivations even without actually belonging to the family. SFOs often opt for a trusted and technically competent person for the role. But families ignore intangibles at their peril. Although hiring technically proficient subordinate staff can fill in small gaps in a non-family manager's skill set, this does not work the other way around. Finding an emotionally intelligent, mature individual with broad knowledge is like discovering a rare diamond.

A family must consider the working environment it is offering and search for just the right candidate to manage the SFO. On the plus side:

- The SFO workplace gives immediate and substantial responsibility to the NFM. This can allow a leader who feels ready to progress but who sees many years or superiors between him or her and advancement in the corporate world to grab the chance to have a real impact.

- The investible funds at the NFM's disposal give him or her gravitas when dealing with asset managers and other external providers.
- An SFO is a unique place in which one can be intellectually challenged, creative and a bit less formal than in other organizations.
- The basic compensation is generally at market level or slightly above, in order to get the right combination of skills and to offset some of the downsides of working for an SFO. It is related to the long-term performance of the organization.
- Quality of life for an NFM in an SFO is head and shoulders above what is possible in many banks, companies and brokerages. As a family office leader noted, "When competing with the big investment houses, you need to find someone who wants a life."[11]

On the minus side:

- SFOs cannot provide an NFM, once in the role, with the vast opportunities for advancement that larger entities can.
- A family office is an unconventional environment. This may sound refreshing in theory, but runs contrary to all prior experiences in the work world.
- Achieving success may not be as easy as it seems. Given the uniqueness of the family office world, what worked for a manager before may need to be tweaked in this new setting.
- The largesse of some investment firm's bonus plans is nowhere to be found in SFOs. So those seeking to maximize their income may be disappointed.

Staffing

As noted in a Merrill Lynch/Campden Research survey, 24 percent of families named recruitment and retention of quality staff as the top challenge for their SFO.[12] Not only is getting the right people on board critical to the performance of the SFO, it is also a key component in the long-term viability of the entity, and hence in the family's vision and purpose. A crucial first step is for the family to decide what qualities it is seeking in staff in order to achieve its objectives. An SFO has much to offer as an employer; but there are limitations, too. Since an SFO tends to have fewer members of staff, employees must act as generalists; there is less support and fewer specialists in an SFO than in a large corporation.

In order to hire the right individuals, an SFO must be willing to interview many candidates and to acknowledge that it may be tapping into less conventional personality types. People who excel in their fields but do not want the constraints typical of the corporate workplace may be prime candidates. It is important to recognize that there must be a rationale for employees to join an SFO, given other options that may offer higher pay and better opportunities for advancement. Trust and core values should be the focus of recruiting efforts.

Case in point: The Owens family

So the Owens family business was separated and evenly divided according to branch (see Appendix A). Bill and family maintained control of much of the property in the enterprise and eventually became involved in real estate development. Arthur operated his portfolio of stores for some time but ended up getting into trouble in the commercial real estate market and lost most of his inheritance.

George's family got supermarkets, liquor stores and real estate. Assuming a structured and perhaps highly cautious approach, the holdings were distributed evenly to George and his wife (25 percent) and to their three children, Richard, Donald and Margaret (25 percent each). Richard operated a successful retail chain for years, but sold out for cash in 1988.

With the proceeds of the sale, Richard formed an investment company and was deciding how his own family of three girls and one son should conduct their family enterprise (see Appendix B). At the same time, Richard's family began constructing a serious family and business governance system.

Rules of the road for setting up a family office

- Structures: No matter whether it is business, family or family office, taking time to think and plan how best to address potential conflicts in your family will help the enterprise thrive. A family office is designed to fill a long-term purpose in the family and in society. Creating governance structures that strengthen the family and enable it to achieve its goals can be arduous work, but pays huge dividends. While outsourcing may be the right call in many circumstances, it should be undertaken carefully and in full understanding of the potential for complexity and risks to confidentiality.

- Process: Learning from others in the field can be helpful in shaping the design and operation of a family office. Use common sense. Think as comprehensively as possible, and for as long as necessary, before taking the first step toward a family office. A little strategy goes a long way. Portfolio management must come front and center. It is the primary reason why most SFOs exist. In-house management of risk parameters, asset allocation, manager selection and yield requirements for investible resources, preferably with a high degree of family involvement, is a must. Let the generation that would experience the most immediate benefits or drawbacks be at the forefront of SFO governance.
- Rules: Establishing rules ahead of time for how the family will conduct its internal dealings and manage its relations with the family office – and with the family business, if it still exists – avoids trouble in the future. It is important that the procedure used to establish the rules be open and inclusive, so all parties feel that they are heard and buy in to the end result.
- Culture/DNA: It could be said that an SFO reaches its pinnacle of success when it preserves both wealth and the family's sense of purpose. Stay true to your family's values and ethos. Otherwise all is lost, no matter how much money you pass along to the next generation. The selection of the non-family manager of the family office is probably one of the most crucial decisions the family will make. This individual must be close enough to the owners to gain an intimate understanding of their motivations and relationships. He or she must acknowledge to himself/herself that he or she will never be a family member, yet must stand as a torchbearer for their deepest desires and goals.

6
The Family Office: What to Keep Your Eye On

> With regard to excellence, it is not enough to know, but we must try to have and use it.
>
> —Aristotle[1]

Perhaps the number one responsibility of a family office is to create a comprehensive overall strategy that ensures family wealth and the ability to fulfill the SFO's purpose for years to come. This is a considerable challenge and, like other issues highlighted in this book, it is murkier and more complex than it looks from the outside. The number one priority and key success factor is clarifying what the family really wants to accomplish and then aligning every other decision to accomplish that one overarching imperative. Although there are many choices, knowing which options are best for your family and family office is less straightforward.

Risk and portfolio management

One of the main functions of a family office is to provide guidance to asset managers on the risk management parameters acceptable to the family and to individual members' risk profiles. Smaller families have fewer choices on investments. But in larger groups investment diversity grows with the increase in diversity of the risk profiles of family-member clients. Again, there is more to this subject than first meets the eye. In addition to establishing the absolute level of risk the family is willing to assume, owning families need to think about how the configuration of their asset management team influences this risk level. Should they select certain managers on the basis of their competency in specific products? Or should they simply divide their portfolio among a number of managers and expect risk diversification to follow?

A couple of other, irrefutable truths impact what looks like a straightforward process. Most obviously, it is difficult to gain real consensus on the general level of risk acceptable to a group of family members who can number in the hundreds. What often happens is that somehow this group agrees on risk parameters, but at the first market downturn everyone suddenly appears to have had unvoiced misgivings about the strategy right from the start, and discord results. It is in human nature not to want to take the financial hit that one's decisions imply.

Furthermore, the family's risk threshold can be a moving target; asset managers and the investment committee need to bear this in mind. As family members leave and enter the group and losses may occur as a result of market movements, the real risk threshold of the family can evolve over time.

Spreading risk

A lot of thought has to be given to diversification, since this process does not occur of its own accord and it is important to understand precisely what it means. For example, does having many asset managers, with a number of them holding the same assets or asset classes, constitute diversification? Practitioners would say not: Although it is not unusual for an SFO to have relationships with 100 or more asset managers, once more than thirty are involved, diminishing returns from diversifying will result. While there is a large universe of potential investments, a much smaller number lie within a particular SFO's stated parameters. Thus, increasing the number of asset managers will not necessarily diversify the family office's holdings. Investment committee and family members must be vigilant in examining and assessing even the smallest details of the portfolio and the constant changes it undergoes as a result of natural market movements.

As part of the SFO's risk strategy, the investment committee needs to formulate a policy on debt. Some family offices will not take on any debt; others are fully leveraged. Issues such as leverage, liquidity and the contractual obligations or restrictions characteristic of some hedge funds and venture capital investments can have an insidious effect and potentially negate hard-won yields. A good strategy is not to over-diversify the investment portfolio and to hold a certain level of cash or near cash positions in order to be able to seize opportunities.

Portfolio selection

The main concern of an SFO in building an asset allocation model should not be return expectations. Instead, the primary guide should be the degree of willingness to absorb a certain level of losses in the portfolio over the long term. Even if this parameter is set on the low side, it should still be possible to generate a reasonable income. Personnel costs, inflation, taxes, costs related to portfolio management and the like will also influence the asset allocation equation.

It is important for SFO leadership to have a historical perspective on finance, as this can help it read and interpret market trends and behaviors. At the time of writing, when the reverberations of the 2008 financial crisis are still being felt, there is a tendency for investors to be more conservative, and some commentators are preaching "doom and gloom." But, as we have seen in the past – and will see in the future – in the long run the market evens out, albeit not without some casualties along the way. When things have been going well for a while, people tend to underestimate the incremental rise in risk. Stocks become expensive, hedge funds increase the lock-up period or fees, or both. This is the time for some prudence.

As Table 6.1 shows, it is obvious that, with potentially higher returns, one has to expect higher volatility. Thus U.S. government bonds, with a 5.2 percent average annual return over a long period, have a standard deviation – which measures historical volatility – of 8.7. Compare this with U.S. small-capital stocks, which have a much higher average rate of return (17.4 percent), but also a higher standard deviation (34.3). Over the almost seventy-year span captured in the table, an investor in U.S. government bonds might have lost 2.6 percent or gained up to 14 percent in any one year. The spread is more marked for stocks, ranging from a loss of 17 percent to a gain of more than 40 percent. The lower standard deviation of an index such as the S&P (around 20) compared to individual stocks (mostly over 20) is due to diversification. This effect will work across the whole portfolio strategy. Diversification usually helps a lot during "normal correction phases," but in the current environment, or during the

Table 6.1 Average rates of return and standard deviation (1926–1994)

Asset class	Average rates of return	Standard deviation
Treasury bills (nominal)	3.7	3.3
U.S. government bonds	5.2	8.7
Corporate bonds	5.7	8.3
S&P 500	12.2	20.2
U.S. small-cap stocks	17.4	34.3

Note: On Black Monday, October 19, 1987, the market fell 23 percent; the standard deviation for that week was 89 percent.

Table 6.2 Average rates of return and standard deviation (1926–2010)

Asset class	Average rates of return	Standard deviation
Treasury bills (nominal)	3.6	0.9
U.S. government bonds	5.4	8.6
Corporate bonds	5.8	7.8
S&P 500	9.8	21.4
U.S. small-cap stocks	11.8	34.1

crash of 1987, liquidity issues become the main drivers in the capital markets. So even long-established relations may break down, as they are overtaken by short-term liquidity needs. Market participants – institutional as well as private – have, for different reasons, to sell across the asset classes, since the portfolio is not providing the annual cash anticipated, and the willingness to provide credit lines disappears. So the SFO has to monitor not only the net investment, but also legally binding commitments in private equity, venture capital and option-relation trades.

Based on the nearly seventy years of capital market performance, families and the SFO can set their own long-term goal, say, with a five- to seven-year investment horizon, and consider at which risk/volatility level they are comfortable. Remember, setting the return expectations to 7 percent or more per annum will shift the portfolio allocation to more risk-affected asset classes such as small stocks, natural resources, private equity and venture capital.

Even if one includes the last fifteen years surveilled in Table 6.2, bonds and stocks showed little difference in standard deviation compared with those in the first example. The lower returns on stocks, however, are a reflection of the 2008 financial crisis and of the couple of years following the bursting of the 2001 dot-com bubble. The message is: Keep long-term relationships in mind and do what is necessary to survive the unexpected. Long-term relationships will probably remain constantly within the bands shown in Tables 6.1 and 6.2.

Endowments

Possible guidance for more active family offices comes from the world of endowments, particularly Ivy League universities. The investment horizon and asset allocation philosophy of universities are in most cases comparable to those in the family office realm. The endowment has to provide, on an annual basis, solid absolute and relative performance. Annual distributions to the owner of the assets are important factors in the investment strategy, both for endowments and for SFOs.

Furthermore, both types of entities must convince owners or administrators that the fees they pay for services have been earned. That is, investment professionals must show those who pay for their expertise that their success is due to excellence, not to the vagaries of the market or, dare we say, to luck. Those who place assets in the care of others want to see themselves doing better than if they had placed their funds in an index fund. The bottom line is that customers must perceive added value from paying for investment advice and management over at least a three-year rolling period.

The annual reports of top universities' endowments – available on their websites – can provide SFOs with guidance and more insights. To balance the views of the investment community, it is also a good idea to consult the websites of the most important central banks, including the Federal Reserve, the European Central Bank and the German Bundesbank. Their views and data collection on the economy and some other insights into current behavior of capital markets are quite useful. (Refer to Appendix D for a further discussion of asset and risk management in the context of large university endowments.)

The role of technology and custodians

The reporting function is an important component of the communication between the organization and its owners. Accounting and reporting systems at the SFO must be technically advanced, perhaps more than would normally be expected at other entities of a similar size. Timely, detailed and customized reporting can result only from maintaining a high degree of technical sophistication and from working with asset managers, custodians and others with computer systems that interface seamlessly with the SFO. In addition to providing individual family members with up-to-date, tailored portfolio reporting – which often has to take into account varying levels of financial sophistication and interest in detail – the SFO needs to aggregate the data so as to present a comprehensive overall picture. In this respect, customization of many elements, reporting included, is a key factor and one of the primary reasons for forming a family office.

Having a relatively large number of external asset managers or custodians may potentially improve the yield and/or the investment mix, but in this scenario accurate and timely reporting can become a complex problem. Portfolio management will also be more cumbersome as the number of parties involved rises. The higher the level of automation in the process, the lower the cost, the fewer the potential errors and the more the staff time that can be spent on weightier issues. In addition, nimble and technologically advanced monitoring and accounting systems can aid the SFO by ensuring and proving compliance with local and international laws and regulations.

The next question is: Should the family office maintain one global custodian or several? Our general advice is that, although to maintain more than one custodial relationship adds to the complexity and probably to the fees of the SFO operation, no one outside provider should glimpse the total picture of the family's holdings. This measure is taken in order to protect two of the family's primary goals in having a family office: privacy and confidentiality.

Doing good well: Philanthropy

Many families incorporate their charitable activities into their SFO, but the nature of these activities has changed dramatically in the recent past. As Melissa Berman, president of Rockefeller Philanthropy Advisors, notes:

> The families we work with today, especially the younger generation, want to more fully understand and participate in their

> philanthropic efforts. They have shifted toward a more global perspective in their giving and are emphasizing the environment, climate change, health and economic development. There are also more stringent requirements for accountability and shorter-term metrics. That is, they are very focused on present day achievements.[2]

The recent worldwide recession has also influenced the level of giving to charities. The American Philanthropic Giving Index produced by Indiana University found that donations were off nearly 22 percent in June 2009.[3] The state of flux of many portfolios has no doubt caused many would-be givers to wait until stability has returned to the capital markets.

The rise of highly involved and motivated young entrepreneurs, flush with cash and looking for worthy projects to invest in, has changed the game for good. No longer do wealthy people embark on long-term, rather nebulous programs of giving to mainstream charities, for which the exact focus of the work and the results can often be rather vague. Rather, these young achievers have begun applying the same principles to their new vocation that made them successful business people. They are not about to write a large check without knowing the specific problems being targeted and the tangible outcomes expected. They like to set milestones and to receive progress reports for individual projects.

These changes in attitude toward accountability and results have given rise to another innovation in philanthropy, which is gaining in popularity. So-called venture philanthropy advocates the adoption of a private equity or venture capital approach to charitable giving; the European Venture Philanthropy Association (EVPA)[4] is at the forefront of this effort. EVPA's members have as their purpose the establishment of funds or other group philanthropy vehicles with tangible goals and high accountability for results.[5]

Many SFOs accommodate and administer the personal philanthropy of family members, as well as helping to direct and focus the collective giving of the group. The design, execution and coordination of family and individual philanthropy are very personal matters, but it is important to allow the next generation to set its priorities, while respecting the methods and preferences of the older generation. The Ivey family of Canada, for example, found that the older generation was committed to improving health care in its hometown. Its children were more focused on wider environmental issues. The common ground they shared was a real passion for contributing to the improved governance of recipient institutions. The Iveys' long experience as donors gave them insights into how advances in organizational operations and strategic planning could make grantee entities much more effective in achieving their objectives. Through this good governance, the Iveys believe they generate far more value for each dollar spent and instill an atmosphere of accountability and excellence that has obvious benefits.

More and more families have begun to seek guidance on how best to spend their philanthropy dollars. Many organizations have sprung up to provide this advice, but we would like to focus on two: Wise Philanthropy Advisors in Geneva and New Philanthropy Capital in London.

Wise Philanthropy takes an analytical and sustainable approach to charitable giving, emphasizing impact and strategy. This organization believes that technical advice, stable financial contributions and access to supportive networks can provide value to both donor and recipient. Grantee institutions must be known as effective quality providers in their field; an exhaustive review of management, transparency and reputation must be undertaken; and measuring performance and project relevance is crucial. Wise's fees are based on a daily rate and allow it to conduct the necessary research and personal visits to potential grantee organizations to help ensure effectiveness and sustainability.[6]

New Philanthropy Capital was founded by former Goldman Sachs partners. They wanted to bring the professionalism and rigor applied to business issues to the increasingly important field of charitable giving. Itself a non-profit-making organization, it charges a daily rate for its services, which center on:

- Clarifying donor objectives and crafting the appropriate philanthropy vehicle
- Educating donors on unmet needs and helping to design a focused program
- Defining how to make effective donations and monitor results
- Analyzing the success of the giving program and its processes.[7]

Here is our advice on how to improve your chances of success in contributing to solutions to some of the world's problems:

- Do not just write a check. Engage in project-driven philanthropy that can have a real impact and may personally involve next-generation members, as well as leaders of the grantee organization and those who ultimately benefit from the family's giving.
- Be vigilant about maintaining efficiency and focusing the family's funds on specific regions or causes that offer the "biggest bang for the buck."
- Consider cooperating with charitable organizations that have knowledge of the geographic area and of the issue at hand and already have operations on the ground.
- Be rigorous in your analysis of potential projects. Cast your net widely. Perhaps consider ten projects and select the best two.
- Emphasize sustainability and robust due diligence in your strategy formulation and assessment of programs and advisors.

Best practices: The Nobel Foundation

Very few families or foundations have been able to manage well their wealth over a long period of time. The Nobel Foundation is, however, an interesting exception. Most people are familiar with the Nobel Prize for excellent achievements, but few know the story behind the scenes. What is the secret of the Nobel Foundation's success? We believe it is a combination of having a clear vision, strong governance rules, good management, good asset management and diversification, good supervision, and flexibility and adaptability.

Alfred Bernhard Nobel was born in Stockholm, Sweden, in 1833, into a family that invested extensively in the education of its children (humanities, natural sciences, languages). He became a successful entrepreneur and traveled the world using his excellent language skills. He created more than thirty companies and, by the time of his death in 1896, he owned ninety-three factories in twenty countries. In total, during his lifetime, Alfred Nobel held 355 patents around the world, in the fields of electrochemistry, optics, biology and physiology. His most famous one was the patent for dynamite, which he received in 1867.

The Nobel Foundation was established and drawn up on November 27, 1895, on the basis of the last will and testament of Dr. Nobel.

It stipulated that the major part of his $9 million estate be set up as a fund, to establish annual prizes for merit in physics, chemistry, medicine and physiology; literature; and world peace – subjects reflecting Nobel's varied interests.

The statutes of the Nobel Foundation were approved on June 29, 1900; they provided for the clear functioning of the Foundation with a board, an administration, trustees of the prize-awarding bodies and an auditing function. The purpose and vision of the Foundation are clearly set out in the statutes:

> The whole of my remaining realizable estate shall be dealt with in the following way: the capital invested in safe securities by my executors, shall constitute a fund, the interest on which shall be annually distributed in the form of prizes to those who, during the preceding year, shall have conferred the greatest benefit to mankind.
>
> (Statutes of the Nobel Foundation, 2005)

The strong governance rules and system, with checks and balances, has served the Nobel Foundation well in its more than a century of existence. Indeed, in accordance with the statutes, the Foundation is to be examined each calendar year by six auditors, including one appointed by the government, one by the prize-awarding bodies and one by the trustees.

The Foundation has also shown great flexibility and adaptability in stipulating that the statutes can be amended – which has happened on several occasions. For example, the capital was invested for a long time only in so-called gilt-edged bonds. However, financial market developments gradually made such bonds less satisfactory as investments and, in the earlier decades, the real value of the fund fell steadily. In addition, the Nobel Foundation was for a long time the largest single tax payer in Stockholm, remitting tax from its inception until 1946, when it was finally exempted from national income and wealth tax, as well as from local income tax. This tax treatment allowed a gradual long-term increase in the size of the Foundation's main fund. Then, in 1953, the government approved a radical liberalization of the investment rules, and amendments to the Nobel Foundation's statutes granted it more freedom to manage its capital independently, as well as a broadening asset allocation, designed to include equities and real estate. Freedom of investment, coupled with tax exemption and the financial expertise of the board, led to a transformation from passive to active management. This was regarded as a landmark change in the role of the Foundation's board.

The Nobel Foundation has also been fortunate in selecting some excellent managers over time. Specifically, Stig Ramel, executive director from 1972 to 1992, invested in real estate but took the wise decision to sell before the real estate market crash of the early 1990s.

Good asset management is stipulated in the Nobel Foundation statutes: "The Board shall ensure that the Foundation achieves a good return and risk-spreading by means of appropriate asset structure and turnover" (Statutes of the Nobel Foundation, 2005).

According to Nobel's will, only direct returns – interest and dividends – could be used for the prize amounts. Capital gains from share management could not previously be used. However, since January 1, 2000, the Nobel Foundation has also been permitted to apply the capital gains from the sale of assets toward the prize amounts. According to these new rules,

> the Board may also use income resulting from sale of Foundation assets for prize-awarding and expenses, to the extent that this income is not needed to maintain good long-term prize-awarding capacity and safeguard the value of Foundation assets *in real terms*.
> (Statutes of the Nobel Foundation, 2005)

Despite periods of rapid inflation, the capital value was not only successfully maintained but also increased. The 1980s and the first half of the 1990s in particular saw a significant increase in the real value of the Foundation's investments. The Foundation was started in 1900 with SEK 31 million. Due to good asset management, the capital at the end of 2009 amounted to SEK 3.1 billon (around $430 million).

Next-generation education

Since an important reason for starting an SFO is to provide a platform for family unity and continuity, many family offices become involved in the education of younger family members. It is in the family's best interests that future generations are educated so as to be capable owners and leaders, and are familiar with how the family office operates. Many SFOs have a mechanism for providing financial support for secondary and/or university education for family members. In this way all members of the next generation have the same opportunities for life-enhancing experiences that will ultimately make them better family members and citizens.

The most critical education a young family member receives is in the home. Parents do much more than they may be aware to encourage a young person either to be passionate about or to withdraw from the family enterprise. This parental influence must be augmented with experiences at the family business, if there still is one, and in formal family governance environments. Depending on the size of the family, education could constitute a minimal expense or a significant expenditure. However, the long-term benefits of a capable family unit cannot be overemphasized. Without wise leadership, vision and devotion to family values, no family group will persist, no matter how much wealth it commands.

Best practices: Bonnier family

The Bonnier family of Sweden has a formalized and structured approach to next-generation education. Its members have called it "Gutkind" – a reference to founder Gerhard Bonnier's original name, Gutkind Hirschel, which he changed when he moved from Germany to Copenhagen, Denmark.[8] Gutkind is aimed at all owners and their children, from 16 to 32. The purpose is to bring together the younger generation and to introduce its members to the business and to one another.

Once a year, Gutkind organizes a theme-based seminar in Sweden, which is followed by a dinner. All expenses are paid, except for air tickets. Every third year, an all-expenses-paid event is organized over several days, where the emphasis is on education and fun. Gutkind web provides news, addresses, pictures, links to family-related sites and an e-mail account (@bonnier.se).

Of particular interest is the focus on the education in ownership of next-generation owners. The consensus is that each generation determines its collective vision as owners and commits to a thirty-year shareholder agreement, as we saw in Chapter 4. The next generation is free to decide upon its own vision. However, the ownership education they receive places heavy emphasis on the culture of the family and the latter's identity as a sixth generation family company, moving into the seventh generation.

The logic of continuity is compelling: If family members are free to decide their own fate, their emotional and motivational commitment to the business will be that much stronger.

Providing a platform for family-member entrepreneurship

One of the main premises of this book is that the cycle of entrepreneurship can be renewed and extended through a family office. Especially if the family company has been sold or the family is so large as to prevent broad participation in managing it, a family office can represent a viable substitute in family leadership development – and this in two ways. As we have already discussed, SFOs give family members the opportunity to bring their gifts and skills to bear in varied capacities in the governance of the family office. And many SFOs expressly provide a forum for encouraging the latent or the obvious entrepreneurial qualities in individuals whose heritage is built on these very traits. As a bare minimum, many SFOs conduct annual family days, when all family members are invited to come to the family office, to hear presentations on its operations and to see how it reflects the values of the founder.

In some SFOs, descendants are encouraged to run their own businesses. Families frequently have programs designed to identify high-potential individuals and to approve venture capital projects in which they are involved. A committee, often made up of both family and non-family members, will regularly review business plans for a new company. Ideas are evaluated by the committee according to industry standards and market rates of return. This activity is not viewed as a "make work program" for the unemployed. The objective is to nurture real entrepreneurship in a family with a rich tradition of pursuing innovation for the benefit of the individual, the family and society.

Communications: External and internal

At first glance, communications might seem to be an odd competency for a private entity. However, the lives of the wealthy and of families who have built high-profile enterprises are of enduring interest to the public. You can try to ignore requests for press interviews, but not for long. In the absence of real information, the press may write its own story. It is far better that they receive a candid account of the family's activities from someone with the authority and knowledge to give it.

Engaging a capable communications expert in the SFO to manage press relations and/or or hiring an external advisor on these matters pays dividends in accuracy and discretion. This is preferable to designating a family member to perform the task, as it can upset the family dynamic if one person is center stage all the time. Without skilful press management, the legacy, reputation and privacy of the family could be placed in peril.

Internal communication is important, too. Keeping family members proactively informed about the SFO's activities is crucial for client satisfaction. Communicating the family's vision and objectives for the organization is a critical task for the administrative team, in concert with the non-family manager. Families report that periodically reiterating the goals and philosophy, as well as sharing the current operating results, of the organization with family members makes things run more smoothly in the long term. Effective reporting becomes more difficult as the complexity of the family office grows.

Forward planning

We have said this before, but it bears repeating: accounting and legal expertise are an important asset within an SFO. The ability to discern one's own financial and legal position and to recognize quality service providers is essential. Maintaining a robust financial function inside the SFO can also help when it comes to monitoring and analyzing expenses. In the rush for earnings, an entity's cost structure is sometimes overlooked.

Another vital function the SFO should take care of in-house is managing and paying taxes for family institutions and individual members. It is just not worth the risk of missing a tax deadline or otherwise running afoul of tax authorities. The l'Oréal heiress Liliane Bettencourt, with allegations of tax evasion and money laundering hanging over her, is learning this the hard way. Make sure tax-paying is done right and by people you know and trust.

In terms of forward planning, the SFO needs to have an emergency plan in place in case of accident or sudden illness in the SFO leadership. Although this may seem like a given if there is an heir-apparent on hand or the future is otherwise assured, it is particularly important in the context of SFOs, since most families tend to underestimate the role of the SFO leader, particularly by comparison with leadership in a family business. This is probably due to several factors: a smaller corporate structure, a limited strategic focus and a lack of corporate history, especially among younger SFOs.

Prenuptial agreements and estate planning documents are crucial to the continuity of the SFO and to family cohesion. The story of shopping mall tycoon Melvin Simon is not new and contains all the traditional elements of a family drama: Second wife, infirm and elderly wealth holder, disgruntled children. Simon signed a new will only seven months before his death in 2009. The revised document left much of his estate to his second wife, while dramatically reducing the inheritance of his children from his first marriage.[9]

With holdings in the estate said to exceed $1 billion and gained through the operation of Simon Property, a major developer of shopping malls in the U.S., there was much to argue over. The dispute over Simon's will arose because of his declining medical condition in the final months of his life, and his children questioned whether he had the capacity to undertake this radical change in the distribution of his wealth. Simon's children are challenging the new will in court, and family unity appears to be under threat. Lesson? Full transparency and disclosure in financial provisions of any kind are key to a healthy, functioning family.

In this context it is worth addressing the particular issues around in-laws. The vast majority of families with businesses and wealth find it difficult to deal with in-laws. We have observed that they are often perceived as intruders. Although in-laws should be considered as part of the family, the most common approach tends to be that they should not necessarily be counted as owners. Most families prefer to pass shares only to blood relatives. This applies typically to older and larger families, who have found it necessary to agree on strict succession rules.

Case in point: The Owens family

Although it did not formally launch an SFO, the Owens family did include many of the features found in a family office in its constitution. First of all, family was defined as direct descendants of Richard and Mary Owens. The constitution also included provisions for the education of future generations, by stating that 85 percent of the cost of high school education for family members would be paid.

The Owens family wanted to encourage the entrepreneurial interests of its members. Proposals for co-investment could be presented to the family business board, which was comprised of family and non-family members. Business plans and cash flow projections were evaluated. A market rate of return was required, as was a workable exit strategy. It was further mandated that the family member seeking this venture capital put in the first 25 percent of equity, to indicate his or her seriousness and confidence of success.

Rules of the road for family office functions

- Structures: Selecting asset managers carefully and establishing wise risk management parameters is absolutely crucial.
- Processes: Defining how to report most effectively is necessary to the successful administration of the portfolio and the SFO alike.
- Rules: Running a successful SFO requires you to follow rules, but with some freedom to create your unique and authentic solutions along the way.
- Culture/DNA: Philanthropy is an area in which the family's ethos and core beliefs are most obviously on display. What you do and how you do it says a lot about what is important to you and how you see the world.

7
Single-Family Office or Multi-Family Office?

> Families are thinking about how to get what they need done in a more effective way. It's not just about efficiency – it's quality as well as cost.
>
> —Maria Elena Lagomasino, CEO
> Genspring Family Offices

In earlier chapters we have seen how challenging it can be to employ both cutting-edge design and efficient administration in a single family office. The difficulty in achieving the goals of a family office can be either eased or accentuated by joining a multi-family office (MFO), depending on your family's situation. As we noted in Chapter 5, an MFO often forms when a family that already has an SFO seeks ways to reduce costs or to retain staff by asking other families to join it. The example of the Bessemer Trust later in this chapter shows that, with a clear mission and good governance principles, many of the benefits of an SFO can indeed be maintained in an MFO, provided that the participating families share the same objectives. However, MFOs do not always gradually evolve from SFOs; some are MFOs from the outset, for example Stanhope Capital (discussed in more detail later in this chapter).

It is said that there are 150 MFOs in the U.S. alone.[1] Europe is lagging behind in terms of numbers because of the significant reliance, until relatively recently, on private banks to perform many traditional MFO functions. In this regard, the main difference between an MFO and a bank is that the former does not push products, and generally charges a flat rate, whereas banks tend to charge transaction fees.

It should also be recognized that an SFO may be larger than an MFO. That is, having more families involved does not necessarily lead to a greater level of investible assets. Many SFOs are mega-corporations in their own right.

As in all things to do with family office, the advantages and drawbacks of each family office situation require close scrutiny and must be weighed carefully. In an MFO, although operating costs may be lower due to economies of scale, services are not provided for free. Furthermore, the involvement of more than one family means that privacy and confidentiality can be compromised. And, inevitably, the values and goals of the families involved will differ. However, this is not to say that MFOs offer a losing value proposition. Rather, this form of group investment may serve the purposes of a family with less start-up capital or without a family leader ready to take on the onerous task of creating an SFO from nothing, or it may serve as a short-term solution to a family business in a transitional phase.

The range of services offered by an SFO and by an MFO can be similar, but the two vary widely according to each organization's design and purpose. There is naturally more emphasis on financial considerations in an MFO, since the participants come from varying backgrounds and sometimes nationalities, and they are not using the MFO as a platform for family unity. An MFO is more of a financial arrangement. Having your own SFO may cost more, but ensures that everything is done according to your family's wishes and in its best interests. However, especially since the financial crisis of 2008, there is a growing tendency for SFOs to consider forming an MFO, in hopes of better returns and lower costs.

Specific items to consider when deciding between an SFO and an MFO include:

- Grouping together with other families in an MFO can provide more opportunities than going it alone. As already noted, families with smaller portfolios may not be able to afford to start an SFO. An MFO operates for profit, whereas an SFO is usually operated as a cost center.
- With which vehicle can we attract the best staff: an MFO or an SFO? The former can generally offer higher compensation because of the larger pool of assets available. The latter offers a

unique working environment, with the opportunity for creativity. Generally career advancement is limited in both types of organizations, as there is often no clear-cut progression plan, but this is not necessarily considered a disadvantage by those who are passionate about working in a family office.

- MFOs may bring economies of scale, but often lack the overarching sense of mission and purpose typical of an SFO.
- The nature of the MFO brings complexity. Because it operates for the benefit of several families, it bears a fiduciary responsibility, possibly requiring audit/registration with the regulatory authorities. Furthermore, the detailed and intricate reporting tasks of an MFO may necessitate more sophisticated technology than is used in an SFO, but this is usually possible because of the MFO's comparatively greater resources.
- Participating in an MFO can be an opportunity to get your feet wet in the field of family office.
- Service levels in an MFO may start out high and erode over time, as the entity is dedicated to the needs and preferences of a group of clients.
- The cost differential between an SFO and an MFO can be substantial. For all costs and fees, including external managers' fees, 1–1.5 percent is considered the standard for MFOs; it can be considerably more for SFOs.
- Relationships may suffer if you invest with friends and family and financial performance declines.
- Especially in an MFO context, advisors suggest that families negotiate a flat fee for services rendered. In most cases fees should not be tied to performance, to avoid potential conflicts of interest and too high risk taking.

When considering whether to join an MFO, Family Wealth Alliance offers the following questions as a guide:[2]

1. How is the service provider owned and paid?
2. What is the ratio of clients per relationship management team?
3. What is the firm's written privacy statement?
4. How is cyber security managed?
5. What services and products do they provide, what don't they offer, and why?

6. Can they help a family train new generations to assume leadership in family governance?

Because there is such variety in the world of multi-family offices, we now look at a couple of examples that illustrate how different families have approached the task of establishing an MFO.

Example: Sand Aire – From family business to SFO to MFO

One of the best-known MFOs is Sand Aire, founded in 1996 and based in the UK. The story began two years earlier, in 1994, when Alexander Scott, aged 35, was appointed chairman of his family's company, Provincial Group. The group's main subsidiary was Provincial Insurance, a mid-sized property casualty insurance firm with a modest overseas presence; other subsidiaries included a small commercial bank. Formed in 1903 by Sir James Scott, Alex's great-grandfather, the business then had premium income in excess of $500 million and some 2,200 employees.

Exploring future options

The insurance industry was going through fundamental change and Alex's arrival coincided with a thorough strategic review, prompted by non-family non-executive directors who were concerned that the insurance sector – and Provincial's position within it – was becoming increasingly vulnerable. Insurance market changes implied more risk: Was this appropriate for a fourth generation, widely held family business? Following a period of intensive exploration of various options, a decision was made to sell the business. The strategic exit was negotiated successfully and the business was sold to UAP of France, which subsequently merged with AXA. Alex commented:

> The decision was taken with heavy heart, but we were clear in our responsibilities to our shareholders (three living generations of my family) and it was apparent that in future we were unlikely to be compensated appropriately for the increasing risks that we perceived we were carrying. We had taken the decision collectively and wished to remain in business together, so my job now was to plan the next steps. I wanted to come up with a contemporary solution, one that was appropriate for an extended family

> with over 90 years' experience in the financial services industry. We wished to respect and respond to our duties as trustees and stewards; it followed that the outcome of our new strategy should emphasize diversification and risk control.
>
> (Interview with Alex Scott)

Alex's research led him to the United States, where he was exposed for the first time to sophisticated SFOs and MFOs. "I was impressed by the caliber of the professionals I met and, when I encountered the MFO model, concluded that this could be suitable for us if I could adapt it to our own needs and circumstances" (Interview with Alex Scott).

With this strategy in mind, the family's board of directors approved a reconstruction scheme that allowed the creation both of a new family investment vehicle and of an investment company to be responsible for managing the family's assets. The scheme also allowed for an appropriate exit for those family members who wished to withdraw. Approximately two thirds of the family's assets were dedicated to a new long-range investment vehicle, the balance being placed in more liquid form.

A successful strategy

Sand Aire was born (the name comes from Provincial's headquarters building), with a core of six professionals and a strategy of evolving from an SFO to an MFO. In fact the existence of some 2000 employee shareholders – who, together, owned 5 percent of Provincial – meant that the firm was managing assets for non-family clients from the beginning. Alex commented:

> The strategy to aim at becoming a MFO was compelling to me and my family: We felt that if we could create a business, rather than a cost center, we could attract, retain and incentivize a high quality team of professionals and, if successful, could not only deliver to my family their investment needs but also create a new family business, one that could eventually be valuable. In this way we could not only deliver an appropriate investment solution on the sale of our business but also build a new one: If we are successful then our generation will have both secured our capital and built upon what we have inherited.
>
> (Interview with Alex Scott)

By 2010, Sand Aire had evolved to become one of a small number of successful, recognized MFOs in London. Alex noted:

> Of course, it took much longer and was much more difficult than I ever envisaged. Just because I could see the attraction of having our assets managed by a skilled, independent team of professionals with no commercial links to financial institutions, it didn't follow that there was an immediate market for our services. We had to build upon our experience in investment management and the financial services industry to create a business with the track record and processes that made it fit for purpose. And we had to wait until wealthy entrepreneurs and families had sufficient confidence and interest in our approach to become our clients. We remain a family business, able to empathize and respond to the multiple issues affecting our clients' success in the context of their wealth, and are also a sophisticated, focused investment management firm. We are able to plan for the long term and offer a rare example of alignment with our clients: We pay the same and get the same as they do.
>
> (Interview with Alex Scott)

With more than twenty other families as clients and with assets under management totaling billions of dollars, the business has now established the momentum originally envisaged.

The combination of dot-com crash and international banking crisis has been painful to most investors, but has also resulted in a fundamental reassessment of risk by most of them. For the wealthiest of entrepreneurs and families, there is now another choice beyond the traditional bank-centered approach, and we are excited by the opportunities we see ahead.

Example: Stanhope Capital – Launching an open MFO

Stanhope Capital is an independent investment firm which provides asset management services to substantial private clients, charities and endowments across the world. Founded in 2004 by Daniel Pinto and Julien Sevaux, the firm was originally formed around a group of five prominent European families aiming at safeguarding and enhancing their wealth by using the best available investment expertise in a conflict-free environment. With offices in London and Geneva and over forty employees, Stanhope Capital is now one of the largest private investment offices in Europe, managing several billion euros for over sixty families, charities and endowments.

From the start, the firm was conceived as an open multi-family office solution, as opposed to being an office built around the needs of a single dominant family. Stanhope's subsequent growth owes much to this founding principle.

The origins

Stanhope Capital came about as a result of the personal experience of its co-founders. While investing their family assets, both Pinto and Sevaux experienced first-hand the structural inefficiencies of the traditional private banking model and, in response, decided to create an entirely new model.

Prior to founding Stanhope Capital, Pinto spent many years at Warburg, advising prominent European families and industrialists on a range of strategic and financial issues. Several of his clients, after selling their industrial groups, delegated the management of their assets to private banks and ended up being seriously disappointed. Pinto and his clients were looking for unbiased investment advice provided by high-caliber professionals. Instead, they found themselves at the receiving end of large product distribution machines mired in all kinds of conflicts of interests and providing poor service. Pinto decided to create an alternative "client-centric" approach and pulled several of his former clients together to create an MFO.

Julien Sevaux, who spent many years working within Lehman Brothers' M&A and private equity divisions, had a similar experience. Sevaux sat on the board of Worms & Cie., the diversified banking and industrial family group. After a liquidity event, his family set about appointing several banks, giving them similar mandates. Sevaux quickly realized the need for a centralized asset allocation and risk management approach that emphasized real diversification across regions and asset classes. He was also convinced that the selection of specialist asset managers, as opposed to banking generalists, would be key to achieving his family's objective and that he would be in a better position to do this within an MFO able to attract and retain the best investment talent.

Bessemer Trust (see below), the oldest and largest MFO in the U.S. and one well-known to the co-founders, took a small stake in

Stanhope Capital at the beginning. It became a strategic partner, providing assistance to Stanhope's research team in certain areas.

Stanhope Capital's philosophy

Neither a bank nor a pure family office, Stanhope aims to bring together the best of both worlds – the high service standards and transparency that can be found in a family office, combined with the quality and depth of investment expertise traditionally associated with a major global bank or institution.

Stanhope defines its mission as being to provide institutional quality investment management to substantial families and charities in a fully transparent environment. It notes the following key principles:

- Wealth management is about advising clients, not about distributing products. Customized asset allocation is implemented within an open architecture framework and with a concern for selecting the best managers wherever they are.
- Independence is a precondition for efficient wealth management. Independence means not having any bias toward specific asset classes, not having an in-house product and not keeping any commission on third-party products acquired on behalf of clients.
- The firm can only serve its clients properly if it can attract and retain the best available investment talent. Investment ideas at Stanhope are generated by the investment team, as well as by an investment committee comprised of both internal and non-executive members. Clients themselves are often a great source of investment ideas.
- Reducing the overall cost of managing a family's assets is a priority. Stanhope uses its critical mass to reduce fees on behalf of clients.
- Stanhope's partners are also clients and are invested alongside other clients. All clients are treated equally: same fee scale; access to the same managers; same level of service.

Stanhope opted for an MFO from the start, and did so for a variety of reasons:

- It is hard to attract and retain the best investment talent in the context of an SFO. Investment professionals with the best track records often want to create their own boutique or to join firms where they are likely to build equity value over time. Also, governance in single-family offices is often a source of concern for these professionals. Who ultimately makes decisions? What if family members disagree on strategy? What if emotions prevail at the expense of rational long-term investment thinking? A multi-family office platform is more likely to be able to address these concerns. MFOs can give a career perspective to the "best and the brightest." MFOs are also able to provide better governance and accountability. Stanhope spends a lot of time with clients to establish clear return objectives, risk parameters, income requirements and tax constraints. But then, the team is able to get on with its work and to remain fully accountable. In SFOs, the lines are often dangerously blurred between the family and the investment professionals.

- In an SFO it is often difficult to have the breadth and depth of expertise required to build truly diversified portfolios. The task of screening and selecting managers across asset classes and regions requires significant resources. Even a team of ten people would be stretched. An MFO, because it has critical mass, may be better placed to meet this challenge. Beyond the issue of resources, an SFO is more likely to look at the world from a single vantage point (the country where the family happens to be based, for example, or the asset class the family is familiar with – often real estate). An MFO can be more global in its approach and more catholic in terms of asset classes.
- Networking is important in the investment world. Stanhope's group of sixty clients from twelve different countries is a constant source of highly relevant information about investment opportunities, managers and the like.

Example: Bessemer Trust – From SFO to MFO

In 1907, Henry Phipps founded Bessemer Trust as his family office. The business partner of American steel magnate Andrew Carnegie, Phipps had amassed a sizable fortune after the sale of Carnegie Steel six years earlier and wanted to create an office that would enhance and preserve his family's wealth while upholding the principles he had always held dear: private ownership, financial prudence and a long-term perspective. For over sixty years, Bessemer Trust – named after the steel-making process so instrumental in Carnegie

Steel's success – served the Phipps family exclusively by providing comprehensive investment, trust and other wealth management services.

The transition

In the early 1970s, however, new challenges emerged for the family office. Expenses were escalating in all areas, particularly in maintaining Bessemer's professional staff and record-keeping system. Added to rising expenses was the need to provide a growing number of individuals – at the time, the Phipps family included some 100 people – with additional services. While the Phipps family was still quite pleased with investment performance and service, costs as a percent of assets under management were high. At that point, the family began to consider the future for their office in light of these increasing hurdles.

With help from McKinsey & Company, the Phipps family explored their options, which were essentially the same ones available to families today: sell (or merge), reduce services, or expand to become an MFO. They rejected the sale as unacceptable, considering that it could result in loss of control, weaker service and the dissolution of the family's unity and legacy. The family also considered reducing services to core capabilities such as investment and fiduciary advisory – thereby eliminating tax, concierge and other services – but this was ultimately ruled out.

Ever since Bessemer was founded, the family reasoned, it had focused on *comprehensive* wealth management; this was the key to the family's financial success, even if such management was expensive. Because the family had the conviction that Bessemer's expertise and experience would be attractive to other wealthy families, consensus formed around creating an MFO. Bessemer took the first step toward developing one by becoming a national bank and trust company in 1974 and began to extend its services to outside families.

Bessemer today

The result of this transition has been a resounding success. Bessemer has now grown to serve over 2,000 clients and to manage approximately $56 billion in assets. For the Phipps family, the decision has been pleasing on a number of levels. The first is the performance and service they have received from Bessemer as clients; by opening Bessemer's doors to new families, the family office was able to grow to the scale necessary to maintain a high level of service and to attract the most talented professionals in order to manage complex matters, ranging from investments to estate planning. The second favorable result has been its financial success. Essentially, the family was able to convert the expense of managing wealth into a significant asset and income stream. Consequently the capital of the business has grown, dividends have increased and the company has continued to attract significant families.

Finally, and perhaps most importantly, Bessemer has been able to maintain the culture so vital to its founding family: a culture centered on private ownership, client service, open communication, independent thinking and an unwavering focus on one business only – private wealth management. This ability to retain key principles and the family's heritage is one of the greatest challenges any family office faces, particularly as the office grows or new generations become involved.

The keys to success

All told, the Phipps family's success in directing Bessemer has stemmed from several crucial decisions the family has made over the last century:

- The patriarch (Henry Phipps) created a family mission statement and a family governance structure that have stood the test of time. Articulating a clear and direct succession plan and determining how the firm was to make decisions provided valuable direction for succeeding generations. Today, each of the five branches of the family is represented on the board by an individual. Younger family members are often added to the board, in anticipation of that branch's director retiring; in this way the next generation is kept engaged with the office's mission.
- *The family kept its history and legacy alive.* Bessemer has become the institution or forum around which the increasingly large family can communicate and share common history. The Phipps family has regular reunions in which they share past stories, introduce new "cousins" and discuss the "family business": Bessemer. Recently, Bessemer employees wrote a Phipps/Bessemer history to help memorialize this family history, and the Bessemer Centennial Reunion in 2007 was attended by over 250 family members.

- *They ran, and continue to run, a successful company*. The family was able to transition from being stewards of wealth generated generations earlier to becoming directors of a new, dynamic business. This allowed new generations to make their own fresh contributions to the family company, as the latter grew and evolved. Moreover, taking on non-shareholder clients gave them comfort that their wealth was being properly and competitively managed, since these families could select any firm and deal with it.
- *They added non-family directors to gain added insights and experience*. By including some directors from outside of the Phipps family, Bessemer ensured that the business would receive important input from people with different business or legal experience. It also helped non-shareholder clients feel more comfortable that the family's interests would not dominate decisions.
- *They focused solely on serving very substantial families*. While some MFOs focus attention, in part, on institutional or smaller retail clients, Bessemer has remained focused on ultra-high-net-worth families.
- *They insisted that shareholder and non-shareholder clients be treated the same*. From the beginning, the family required that all clients have equal access to investments, planning and advice while receiving equal levels of service.
- *They demanded client service at the same level as in an SFO*. The hallmark of an SFO is an extremely high level of service, which MFOs can lose sight of without the proper direction. Bessemer remains committed to keeping the client-to-staff ratio low – today it is 3:1.
- *They attracted, incentivized and retained professional management and staff to achieve client goals*. The success and sustainability of any office depends on how well it can build a team of committed professionals. For many SFOs, the greatest challenge has been to attract and retain a professional staff that maintains the service mentality required by wealthy families, yet delivers investment and financial expertise that competes with that of the best Wall Street firms. By becoming an MFO and continuing to grow its client base, Bessemer allowed for the financial success necessary to provide competitive compensation and to offer career opportunities for young professionals. Two factors aided Bessemer's success: management has an ownership interest, and compensation is tied to client-centric goals, not merely to profitability.

Rules of the road for choosing the right family office for your family

- Structures: If neither an MFO nor an SFO suits the needs of your family, emphasizing family governance can still help promote cohesion and continuity in their absence. The family can still support philanthropic endeavors and next-generation education and thereby advance its own entrepreneurial tradition.
- Process: A thorough evaluation of your options should be undertaken prior to any action. Meet extensively with the representatives of any MFO you are considering joining. Talk to your friends. You must be comfortable with your primary contact at the MFO, as this is an important and probably long-standing relationship, critical to your family's wealth and future. You may also want to vet the risk management professionals at the MFO, as well as the relevant asset managers.
- Rules: Understand your exit options. Is there a tie-up period? Liquidity calls? What is your level of input on major decisions of the MFO: Some? None?
- Culture/DNA: We think an SFO is the best way to go in providing a solid foundation for family heritage and beliefs for decades to come, irrespective of whether the family business exists or not. But, in certain situations, an MFO can fulfill the needs of some families and give these families time to consider their options.

8 The Cycle of Entrepreneurship Continues

> People will not look forward to posterity who never look backward to their ancestors.
>
> —Edmund Burke[1]

We have traced the evolution of families in business from the first inklings of the founder's great idea to a growing family business and finally, with luck and hard work, to the family office. From there, the next generation's hopes and dreams are on the line as the family supports the renewal of the cycle of entrepreneurship started many years ago.

Through these chapters we have looked at what is particular to the entrepreneur, the pursuit of a thriving business, the continuity of family tradition and what the family does to initiate this cycle of achievement once again. Each stage has its own specific elements, but there are also a few general principles that are applicable in all scenarios, from entrepreneurship to family business to family office and back to entrepreneurship again.

Entrepreneurship

The main lessons at the entrepreneur stage resonate throughout the life cycle of the family. The entrepreneur develops the vision through an often difficult process of trial and error, which leaves a deep imprint on the developing family culture. Understanding that any venture needs initial structure, rules and processes, but that all of these are subject to evolution over time is fundamental to the system as a whole.

The entrepreneur also defines and lives the values, "walking the talk" and demonstrating leadership. Future generations interpret these values and give them meaning in their own way, as heirs. Continuity is the big issue for the entrepreneur. His intensive personal experience and identity overlap with the business he has created – "my baby." This makes it difficult for him to imagine and to plan for a future in which his business and the next generation owners have different needs and a different leadership.

Family business

As a new generation enters the business, there is a need for a new structure. Truly to understand and appreciate the present – and the future options – it is imperative to go back to the beginning and ask the question: Who are we? There is no substitute for a healthy family and corporate culture, respect for self and others and the freedom of individual choice and authentic expression.

It is also essential to gain clarity on strategy, first in terms of ownership, then in terms of the business. The next generation needs to decide whether to retain, modify or overthrow the "old" strategy and create its own. What do we want – and do we want to do it together?

In order to work out "How are we going to decide – together?," the next generation needs to put governance structures in place. The appropriate forums for decision-making are needed at each level: The family needs a family council to create a family constitution; the owners need an owners council to decide on asset and resource allocation; and the business has a board of directors which makes the relevant decisions and gives direction to management.

No family can journey into the future together without mastering the complex skills of communication, compromise, maturity, facilitation of healthy conflict resolution and inclusivity. As the company grows, so does the number and diversity of its staff. The value of outside independent voices who are motivated by nothing other than professionalism and community cannot be overestimated. With family and non-family managers alike, the only valid guiding principle is merit. Keeping the owning family involved – as responsible owners and, in a perfect world, as competent managers – is a good way to make sure the corporate culture remains compelling, meaningful and focused in the right direction.

Family office

The message we have been trying to communicate is this: A family office is an excellent option for families who have garnered significant wealth, grown to a certain size, experienced substantial geographic or generational dispersion and seek to stay together as a potent force. A family office may be critical in achieving this goal, particularly if the family business has been sold. Even if the family firm remains intact, a family office is generally a good idea, since not all members of a growing family can work in the business. There must be a means for self-expression and demonstration of commitment to the common good in another way as well. The diverse work of a family office means that many attributes and competencies may be employed for the good of the family, for example in philanthropic endeavors that support common social and environmental values. The family office provides a reason to pull together as a team and a vehicle for future growth.

This is not the easiest time in history to consider forming a family office. Many of the primary justifications for a family office may appear less robust than just a short while ago, with the financial industry reeling from the effects of the 2008 financial crisis. Some of the consequences of the economic fallout that we see as relevant include:

- Confidentiality and reputation rank now as top considerations in assessing external service providers, replacing a singular focus on yield.
- There is a renewed appreciation for smaller, independent asset managers.
- Long-term relationships and trust have again come into fashion.
- Risk assessment and proper due diligence are essential.
- Philanthropic funding has declined, in line with reduced portfolio values.
- Smaller SFOs tend to look for cost and other benefits by turning to MFOs.

Coming full circle: The family office as a platform for encouraging entrepreneurship

The old wisdom was that, when a family had made it, it should *lock in the capital*, to ensure that it would last. Family members/beneficiaries only received a small yearly dividend and could not touch the capital, to avoid eroding it. For many families this may have worked initially, but, after the death of the older generation, fights often broke out and the management of assets by banks or trustees started to be called into question; few family businesses survived even fifty or seventy years.

Today, fostering entrepreneurship in future generations is a better way of keeping wealth – and hopefully the family – together over longer periods of time. Families with wealth need to do everything in their power to counteract the natural tendency for the entrepreneurial spirit to dissipate gradually in the younger generations. Although one might like to think that the character traits that fuel the desire to start one's own business are innate, they can be dulled by the lack of urgent financial need or of the desire to improve one's standard of living. It is ironic that, if the original entrepreneur succeeds in his or her quest to found a long-lasting enterprise, his or her children may, through lack of financial worries, be pushed in the opposite direction. They often do not have the hunger for success, or the enthusiasm for a product, that their father or mother had. However, the path to new entrepreneurship can be paved by the family office. It keeps the business spirit alive in the family and enables the development of new ventures.

Perhaps the most important obligation of successors is to develop themselves as competent owners, so that they may be able to uphold their responsibilities to past, current and future generations of their family. In this regard, an educated ownership base is essential. While many families pressure the next generation into taking university courses that would be useful to the family business, it is probably more effective to support financially the education of next-generation family members in their field of choice, where their talents and interests can come to the fore. Having said that, one can go too far in the opposite direction by sponsoring a host of children in rather nebulous pursuits. Above all, balance is essential, and the link to a tangible past should be encouraged. The family's way of living should never stray too far away from its roots; otherwise rot sets in and wealth erodes.

Beside education, next-generation family members should play their part – as family governance rules and bodies allow – in overseeing the collective wealth and in contributing to advances in family governance mechanisms. The family's philanthropy can provide growth opportunities and managerial experience for future generations. Taking part in the family's activities affords younger family members the chance to try their hand at formulating initiatives, managing projects and seeing them through to completion: a good training ground, indeed, for next-generation entrepreneurs.

Risk-taking, in particular, should be stressed in a young person's development. In some sense, the wealth generated by their elders may have removed that element of danger and, with it, an essential learning opportunity from their lives. But new ventures cannot be launched without the ability to assess risk accurately and to live with uncertainty. A healthy dose of risk tolerance is critical to managing a firm into the big leagues and for the long term.[2] "Protecting the downside" is how Richard Branson expresses it: "One needs to be sure before one can be bold, try new things and still afford the cost if the project doesn't work out."[3]

Continuity through the generations is too frequently addressed from the wrong end: attempting to perpetuate finance and business structures. Family often comes as an afterthought, with the implication that, if there is money and business, the family will – and should be – sufficiently motivated by this. A study conducted on Swiss family businesses[4] revealed, however, that the key drivers for continuity, as seen by the owning families, are, in order of importance:

- Independence
- Entrepreneurial spirit
- Passion for the business
- Source of income
- Jobs for the family.

Time and again, we have observed this disconnection between business-owning families' intentions – as expressed in this research – and the actual implementation of continuity plans. They are all too often built on perpetrating financial and business structures that are forced on future generations of family owners. We are convinced of the multiple and long-term benefits of "managing through culture," whereby next generation members are wisely prepared for the options that lie ahead in their generation and are ultimately given the responsibility to decide by and for themselves.

Example: Hartwall – From "old" to "new" as a family in business

The following example highlights the case of an older and larger European family having exited its business and constructing a new shared platform.

The sixth-generation Hartwall family has been in the beverages and brewing business, from its base in Finland, for over 170 years. In 2007 the family exited the business as the result of a takeover. It found itself in a new situation and made several key strategic decisions:

- Keep together: Together we can do more than on an individual basis.
- We are an entrepreneurial family: We have no ambition to be an institutional investor, and we will maintain the entrepreneurial spirit.
- Continuity: The capital is a loan from our children and we have a long-term view with no exit strategy.

The family process that achieved the shared vision outlined above then became a business process, as a governance structure was created (advisory board and investment board) and a non-family CEO was appointed. The strategy was defined as:

> The strategic aim of Hartwall Capital is to enhance the value of the inherited wealth of its owners in a sustainable and ethical way that enables the members of the family to successfully pass on their legacy to future generations.
>
> (Family presentation at FBN Summit, Amsterdam 2009)

The approach to business involvements was segmented into family businesses, industrial investments and financial investments. The family uses regular communication in order to stay together and to address the new challenges of being involved in several new industries.

Example: From "old" to "new" – As an individual next-generation member

The following example highlights a transition from family office to entrepreneur: In this relatively small European family, the father is a highly successful industrialist who created a sizable SFO after the sale of the large family business. The father's intention was to create a strong foundation and platform, to allow for a professional approach to managing the family's wealth and, furthermore, to give the next generation opportunities to pursue their own individual careers. The family values are strong: meritocracy, excellence, pursuit of detail, honesty and humility. Its motto is: "Do the best in what you do, but do something." A strong international education and work experience are seen as the "financial passport" to allow each family member to own wealth responsibly. The father treats the children equally and offers them the opportunity to draw against their future inheritance in order to fund an active entrepreneurship project – either a start-up or a business acquisition. Certain ground rules have to be observed: The project has to stand on its own merits, be supported by an independent team of family advisors and be acceptable to banks for the granting of loans. The children are allowed to fail and try again. But they bear the losses.

The thirty-year-old daughter, having worked for three years in various departments of the family office and having obtained an MBA, decided to take up this offer and to search for a business to acquire and run along with her husband, who has substantial management experience. They decided on the following selection criteria: location, substantial size (in accordance with the available capital), cutting-edge and innovative technology, medical industry with a human touch. The search was supported by the network of the family office, but was conducted exclusively on the daughter's initiative. Over two years, more than 200 companies were looked at. Due diligence was exercised. The daughter was cautious in her approach, as one of the incentives was to create wealth at a higher rate than the family office.

This entrepreneurial venture remains as part of the daughter's personal wealth, outside the family office. Her intention is to become actively engaged in building this business in the long run: to buy and hold. It may become a family business in another generation.

Her 28-year-old brother, meanwhile, has rounded off his education and experience in the field of private equity, working for an outside firm where he can follow the process and mechanisms of investing in private businesses with an exit target. He has gained solid insights, which will be important and meaningful for his future:

> The knowledge we gather individually will professionalize our approach to ownership and assist the ongoing innovation of the family office platform.
>
> (Interview with the family)

Case in point: The Owens family

The story of the Owens family has been a good partner in our journey through the cycle of entrepreneurship, family business and family office. All three of these areas were major sources of trouble as well as delight for different generations of the Owens family. Its members enjoyed early success; endured deep-seated pain, caused by lack of communication and of generosity of spirit among themselves and the leadership; and yet somehow they emerged wiser and stronger.

It was important that someone took control of a situation which had been ignored, but which ultimately threatened family harmony and wealth. Richard courageously stepped up to take on the mantle. The company had limped along somehow, despite discord in the family. But someone had to stop the destructive ways of the second-generation board members, which had already begun to spread to the younger Owens. Richard called the bluff of the older generation and took his substantial talent for business elsewhere when family members could not look beyond their own shortcomings for the good of the group. He learned a painful lesson about how indispensable governance and accepted practice and process are to any endeavor, and especially to a family enterprise.

One of the first things Richard did when he struck out on his own, with his own nuclear family, was to establish a mechanism for the recognition of entrepreneurial talent and enthusiasm in family members and to find a meaningful way to encourage and support them. The Owenses' story shows us that, if we learn from our experiences, positive and negative alike, we still have a chance to create something long-lasting and satisfying.

Rules of the road in entrepreneurship, family business and family office

- Structures: Good governance is the key to the whole system. Establishing sound and flexible governance will serve the family well throughout its life cycle.
- Process: Although your eyes are, rightly, set on the big picture, the details must not escape your attention. Macro-level thinking does not supplant the need to get things like effective communication with the family right. Providing the platform for the next generation to grow and prosper in accordance with your core beliefs is an awesome responsibility, but also an honor and a duty.
- Rules: Rules are essential, but they are no substitute for a learning-oriented approach. If you are fortunate enough to be a multi-generational family in business, you will no doubt periodically need to assess, adjust and move forward. Beware: a sustainable future requires the ability to manage culture more than it requires a large number of rules.
- Culture/DNA: Understand enough about your family character and dynamics to know if a business or family office is viable into another generation.

9
How It All Comes Together – The Long-Term View

> Every right implies a responsibility; every opportunity an obligation; every possession a duty.
>
> —John D. Rockefeller, Jr.[1]

Over the course of this book we have explored many issues relating to the concept of the cycle of wealth. We have looked at the beginning of the creation of wealth – most typically by entrepreneurs. When the family grows – either in the same generation or in the next – the business becomes a family business. Over time, business considerations are enlarged to include an ownership platform.

The original business may still be the main source of revenues, it may have seen the addition of other businesses, or it may even have been divested. The family's way of thinking must shift to ownership matters and private wealth preservation in order to safeguard and protect what has already been achieved. The right balance between conservation and growth needs to be found. This is where the family office can be of help: in providing a structured approach to managing private wealth. Then the focus must be on preparing the next generation for a responsible ownership, in order to prevent the erosion of what past generations have built.

Encouraging a healthy understanding of business management and entrepreneurship is the best guarantee of survival into future generations (see Figure 9.1). The underlying philosophy is compelling: Each generation inherits what has been created by past generations of family, benefits from it and adds value to it, so that future generations can, in turn, take advantage of what has been accomplished

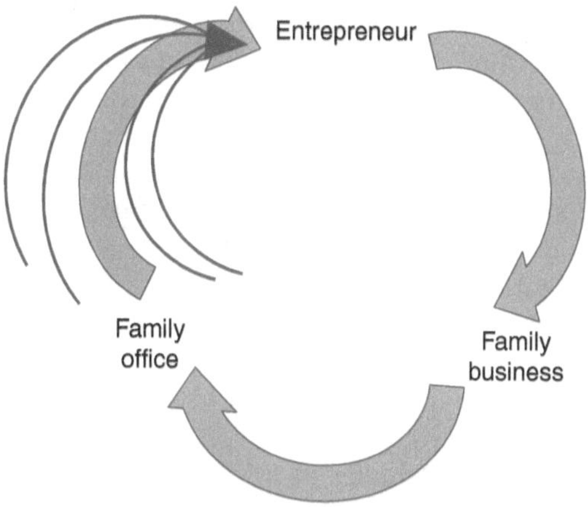

Figure 9.1 Cycle of wealth

by their forefathers. Thus the cycle of wealth can become a continuous renewal process. The owners and the family become stewards for future generations.

The general principles that seem to crop up in a serious discussion of families in business at any stage of the cycle are as follows:

- Communication is of the essence.
- Aim for excellence in governance.
- Open, candid, inclusive family engagement is vital.
- "Failing to plan is planning to fail."
- Recognize the power of structure, process, rules and corporate and family culture.
- Embrace the uniqueness of family business – with its emphasis on incremental growth, on unique approaches that work but make sense only to business families, and on achieving a higher purpose.
- Risk is part of living and, indeed, is inherent in every aspect of business and family.
- Be who you are, as individuals and family. That's the way it turns out anyway!

Creating, managing and keeping wealth for future generations is a noble mission. Being able to control ownership and management can lead to superior results and benefits for the broadest range of stakeholders. In every generation, strong and visionary leadership at family, ownership and business level is a must. An enlightened approach with a healthy sense of humility for the task is a prerequisite. Although thinking ahead into the next generation might seem a daunting exercise, it should be thinking ahead *for* the next generation, anticipating their potential needs in a changed environment. The key task of each generation is twofold: First, to ensure sustainable family wealth and a sustainable business strategy in its own generation; second, to lay the groundwork to enable the next generation to make the best possible decisions for an ownership vision of its own. This requires a carefully balanced approach to guiding and enabling the next generation. We have given examples of successful, multi-generational families in business that have followed this path. Strategies, governance structures, family offices – these are the mechanisms which allow for wisely creating, managing and keeping wealth.

If there is one single conclusion to be drawn at the end of this book, we would express it as follows: Success *can* be planned!

Appendix A
Original Owens Family Tree

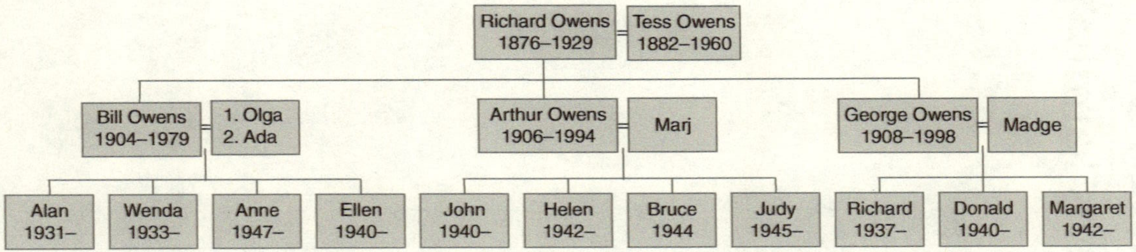

Source: Derived from company information.

Appendix B
Owens Family Tree 1995

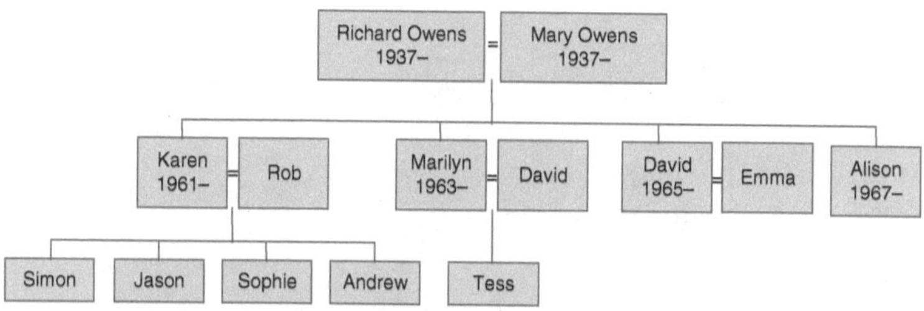

Source: Derived from company information.

Appendix C
Scope of Services for a Large Single-Family Office

Asset Management

Individual advice and portfolio management

Asset allocation
Manager selection
Liquidity planning
Rebalancing
Risk management
Global custody/custody

Individual reporting

Personal accounting and reporting
Auditing

Tax and Legal

Tax advisory and tax return filing

Strategic tax advisory and implementation
Cross-border constructions
Tax return filing

Estate planning

Family contracts/antenuptial agreements
Succession planning
Testaments/gifts/donations/foundations/rusts
Executorship of wills/trusteeship of trusts

Other legal advice and services

Citizenship issues
Legal advisory vis-à-vis central or local authorities
Legal advisory on re-establishment of private businesses
Real estate contracts
General legal advice

Media Communications

Press relations
Trusted media relations

Banking and Insurance

Banking

Banking and clearing
Account statements, account monitoring
Account administration/bookkeeping
Payments and transfers
Financing, loans, mortgages
Cash advances, including foreign currencies
Credit cards

Insurance

Insurance selection
Property and car insurance
Health insurance
Life insurance
Liability insurance
Insurance maintenance and claim handling
Personal pension plans

Private Housing

Property selection
Purchase and sale management
Property administration
(Pre-purchase) surveys
Supervision of building and alteration works
Alteration permits (monuments, zoning, neighbors)

Security

Individual servicing

Surveillance of residence, schools, commuting routes
Electronic surveillance of residence and cars
Security advisory towards private housing
Domestic staff screening

Group servicing

Contacts with the police
Personal data storage and files

Ransom policy
Executive protection
Car-jacking training
Kidnap-avoidance advisory
Crisis management/contingency planning

Personal advisory

Medical services
Individual coaching (mental, lifestyle, family and marriage issues, crisis management)
Education (school selection, college advisory, career)

Concierge

Travel

Travel planning and arrangements
Visa, passports, drivers' licenses

Sourcing of services

Negotiation of service contracts (telecom, utilities, communities)
Car sales and purchases, registration, lease and rental, drivers
Domestic staff, screening, hiring, administration, pension
Other

Relocation

Removals, international transfers, white good purchasing
Pet services (e.g. registration, transportation, quarantine)

Other services

General secretarial services
Private IT services
Bill payments
Forwarding, fax and mail services
Art services (sale/purchase, insurance, shipment/auction, representation, export clearance)

Philanthropy

Education
Guidance
Selection
Execution
Structuring
Reporting

Source: Hakan Hillerström.

Appendix D
The Yale/Harvard Model of Endowment Investment: The Importance of Asset and Risk Management

For many in the family office world, the gold standard in investing is exemplified by the endowments of two Ivy League universities, Yale and Harvard. For many years, both of these institutions experienced remarkable short- and long-term success in growing the portfolios that the universities depend on as an important component of their annual operating budget. As recently as the 1980s, the endowment funds were invested relatively conservatively and mostly in publicly held stocks and bonds.[1] But, almost inevitably, the push came to squeeze more and more yield out of the already healthy endowments.

Harvard has the largest university endowment in the world, totaling $26 billion at the 2009 financial year end (FYE), although this was down from a high of $36.9 billion the previous year.[2] Yale's portfolio was a substantial $16.3 billion at FYE 2009, but it had also fallen from $22.9 billion at FYE 2008.[3] Harvard and Yale are, both, top-flight educational institutions, and both of them benefit from substantial endowment funds provided by alumni and other donors. However, their paths have diverged substantially in endowment investing over the years.

Perhaps the starkest difference is in the overall design and approach employed by the two universities. David Swensen has headed up Yale's endowment, investing for over two decades, and he has really defined the "Yale Model" of investing. When he joined Yale from Wall Street, endowment portfolios were more "plain vanilla" than they are today. But Swenson was a proponent of alternative investments in order to boost the performance of the endowment.[4] Swensen, a Yale alumnus himself, had early success with investing in non-traditional assets, such as private equity, hedge funds and commodities. The idea took hold and soon many Ivy League and other universities were configuring their portfolios similarly.

Harvard took a different approach, setting up the Harvard Management Company – a wholly owned, yet independent entity whose job is to manage the endowment. The institution has come under fire over the years for the extremely generous compensation packages paid to its investment pros.

But what may have been an idea with some merit went too far in the heady days of the early twenty-first century. As we all know, no excess was too big and no business model too far-fetched to be turned away by the markets. In this environment, Yale and Harvard built large endowments through investments that donors would probably never have envisioned for their gifts. It dawns on the casual reader, if not on the university board and investment managers, that putting the gifts of dedicated alumni to work in forestry or in highly technical arbitrage vehicles could be construed as a bit cavalier. We wonder whether the whole endowment industry did not get caught up in the same game of excess as Wall Street, forgetting its prime purpose of providing a stable income stream to its institutions. In any case, the two schools, and especially Harvard, became increasingly dependent on earnings from the endowment for its operating budget.

Table D.1 illustrates the performance of the two endowment funds over the years. Both Yale and Harvard have experienced notable gains in the value of their portfolios in the recent past. But, with the onset of the 2008 recession, these endowments suffered losses on a par with the 28.2 percent decline in the S&P 500 over the year ending June 30, 2009. One might suggest that all these sophisticated machinations did not help the cause of sustainable higher earnings and in fact caused more harm, in the form of the illiquidity of private equity and hedge fund investments, and even of additional funding required by some venture capital investments in the portfolio.

The figures shown in the last line of the table are from a benchmarking service for non-profit-making entities provided by Wilshire Associates' Trust Universe Comparison Service (TUCS). Custodians holding assets on behalf of tax-exempt portfolios contribute data on risk levels, asset allocation and other characteristics to the TUCS database. Endowment managers can subscribe to this service in order to gauge performance, investment distribution and risk relative to peer institutions.

Most universities establish a policy portfolio, which is basically a target asset allocation model approved by the board and given as a guide to asset

Table D.1 Endowment performance

Average returns FYE (June 30, 2009)	**1 year (%)**	**5 years (%)**	**10 years (%)**
Yale	24.6	8.7	11.8
Harvard	27.3	6.2	8.9
TUCS Median	18.2	2.5	3.2

Source: Harvard Management Company Endowment Report, September 2009; The Yale Endowment, 2009; "Yale University Releases Endowment Figures," news release, 22 September 2009.

managers. Harvard, in response to the tremendous loss in endowment value, made some changes. It is widening the hybrid investment model it employs, and one third of the portfolio will henceforth be managed internally. The endowment will make flexibility and de-leveraging a priority. Some incremental changes were noted in the FY 2010 policy portfolio. The endowment will seek to have less exposure to hedge funds and commodities and slightly to increase cash holdings.

However, a shift to cash highlights an Achilles heel in the SFO world. Does a family office make sense if your assets are concentrated in cash? Active management of the portfolio in order to achieve returns higher than those possible from cash or indexed assets is one of the main reasons for founding an SFO. The bottom line is: There needs to be a reason beyond money that gives the family office meaning and purpose.

So the lesson seems to be that focusing solely on yield and putting other dimensions of risk on the back burner, if not totally out of the kitchen, can end in disaster. Casting a critical eye on other variables is essential if one is to protect SFO assets. For instance, diversification can be an illusion if you have numerous asset managers. A truly holistic approach to portfolio management is the best way to face any potential economic event.

Appendix E
Case Study: Four Generations of the Owens Family (A)

IMD INTERNATIONAL

The Owens family started in business almost 100 years ago. It was 1906 when the family patriarch, Richard Owens, used lottery winnings and the majority of his savings to purchase his first general store in Wollombi, Australia. For him, this step was more than just the realization of years of hard work. It meant that he could begin a business that fulfilled his plans and vision for his family. These plans were based on his years of experience working in local stores and on his instinct about how things could change in the future. He firmly believed that business was built on mutual respect, trust and attention to customer needs.

Third-generation Richard Owens understood just what his grandfather meant. He had inherited the founder's entrepreneurial spirit and interest in the fast-paced world of retail. But the company had long since gone astray from this model of one strong man leading the way. Now it was up to Richard to set things right.

Richard Owens: Business and family leader

Background

Richard chose the town of Wollombi, with its relatively large rural population, for his first location, largely because of its promising customer base. Competition for this clientele was essentially nonexistent and Richard could have prospered with a minimum of effort, by simply supplying the town's basic needs. But, in accordance with his core values, Richard provided customers with a full array of products. Selection was not the only highlight of the store. The latter boasted convenient hours, and delivery was provided for those unable to make the trip to town. Credit was advanced and debt was often settled in trade. Residents rewarded Richard's tireless service through loyal patronage.

Although many businessmen in the early 1900s would have been satisfied with this level of success, Richard had more ambitious goals. He believed that outstanding service was not enough to ensure prosperity; price competition would become a greater issue in the future. After long hours of studying the market, Richard decided that his best chance of increasing profits was through higher volumes. With a sufficient increase in sales, he could negotiate purchases directly with manufacturers and bring more to the bottom line.

Richard's business philosophy and family life were closely interwoven. The honesty and persistence that were endemic to his work were a part in everything he taught his children. He and his wife Tess had three sons. Bill, the oldest, was born in 1904. Arthur and George followed. (Refer to Figure E.1 for the Owens family tree.) Education was of primary importance, and involvement in sports and music were actively encouraged. The brothers grew up to be very supportive of each other, and each took great pride in being a member of the Owens family.

From the time they were able to help, the children were given duties in the store. They were taught how to work fast and accurately and they were encouraged to greet every customer with a smile. While the family worked, Richard continually planned for its future and made sure that his boys understood his vision.

Expansion

It soon became apparent that Wollombi could no longer support Richard's long-range plans for the business and the family. In 1919, after a careful search, Richard purchased a general store in Islington. Its location on the route connecting important cities offered a thriving and growing customer base. The Owens' business concept remained essentially unchanged, and the new store still provided a wide selection of merchandise and reliable service. Credit continued to be extended readily when a customer's finances did not allow cash and carry. The family became heavily involved in the community. Richard's business approach proved to be even more successful than before. The customer base grew so rapidly that in 1920 Bill, at age 16, was called home from boarding school to work full time in the store. Arthur soon followed in 1921 and George in 1923.

The operation grew according to plan, and in 1926 the business was incorporated as Richard Owens Pty. Ltd. Richard organized the ownership structure so that he held the only voting share. Non-voting shares were divided equally among his wife and sons. His intent was to instill a sense of financial responsibility for the family and to have all profits distributed without favoritism. In the years that followed, the credo of the Owens family could be summarized thus: All were responsible for the business and all shared equally in its rewards.

Also in 1926, at Bill's behest, the Owens family formed the first grocery-buying group, Wholesale Traders Pty. Ltd. Price discounts were passed on to customers, and the business prospered. In 1927 the business expanded. The family and business did well until 1929, when Richard Owens unexpectedly died.

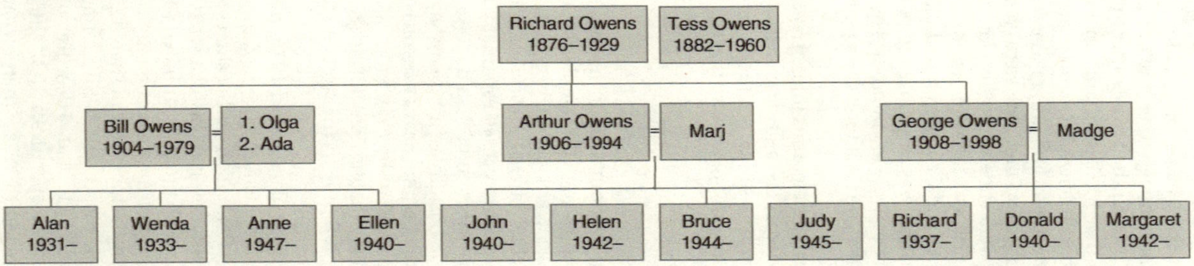

Figure E.1 Owens family tree

Source: Derived from company information.

The second generation

The Depression and the division

Following Richard's example, company ownership was divided among Tess and her three sons. Voting control, however, was held by the three siblings. Because of his seniority and initiative, Bill led the enterprise. His success with Wholesale Traders had encouraged his entrepreneurial tendencies, and he was determined to lead the company the way his father had done. The other brothers took positions as company directors.

The onset of the Great Depression, ironically, provided tremendous opportunities for the Owens' business. Other storeowners, who were unable to persevere, looked for a chance to sell their stores for whatever they could. Many approached the brothers for help, knowing their history of assisting those in financial trouble. With their father's advice ringing in their ears, the three men mortgaged everything they owned in order to buy what assets they could.

In 1930 the business declared its first loss and, with the possibility of bankruptcy now a daily reality, nothing mattered more than keeping the business afloat. As the business grew, a clearer delineation of responsibilities was needed. Bill, who had inherited his father's talent for inspiring loyalty and hard work from his employees, assumed the ever-expanding managerial duties.

During his years at the store, Arthur had gradually taken on all the administrative functions and, as the Depression worsened, his role became increasingly important and stressful. Arthur had developed an obsessive attention to detail. His relationships with employees suffered.

George became a store manager, directing the work of many older employees. His determination was obvious, and before long he was accepted and eventually supervised six stores. The fact that he was able not only to survive but also to prosper in such a challenging position inspired and invigorated George. He actively began to seek new hurdles and enjoyed taking risks.

The conflict

The divergent work attitudes of George and Arthur soon began to create conflict between the two brothers. George's life was a very positive experience; each day was filled with new challenges and exciting responsibilities. This, understandably, made him eager to continue to expand the business. Arthur, on the other hand, spent his days in a secluded room, faced with the reality of growing debt. The numbers constantly reminded him of how burdened he and his brothers were. They could lose everything, and during the Depression there was no one to go to for help. Arthur did not support George's ambition and vision, and even seemed to resent it.

Since the decision-making power in the organization was equally distributed among the brothers, some degree of family harmony was necessary. Bill was thrust into the role of peacemaker. But he was uncomfortable in this role, and uncomfortable with conflict. Personal problems compounded his difficulties. Looking to the business for peace and stability, Bill withheld any sign of disagreement at work. Consequently the antagonism between George and Arthur was allowed to continue unchecked.

This conflict was kept under control for many years by the stabilizing presence of Tess. She got up early every morning to make sure the porch was swept and the shop, above which she lived, was in order. The brothers joined her for meals each day. It was these rituals that kept the sense of family alive.

By 1939, Richard Owens Pty. Ltd. was prosperous. All three men were married, and Bill and George had a son each. Despite the family squabbles, the company was proving to be successful against tremendous odds. Just when things seemed to be on the right (though tenuous) track, another major hurdle appeared.

The fighting continues

Bill, who had been in the military reserves, was given three days' notice to report for active duty in World War II. He had always enjoyed working with the army and particularly relished the chance to escape from his increasingly difficult marriage. The separation soon led to divorce. Before long he reached the rank of lieutenant colonel and enjoyed the power of his position. Life in the military agreed with Bill, and he soon met and married his second wife.

Just before Bill was due to lead his troops into war, the military command structure changed and a general took over. Effectively stripped of his power, Bill was saddled with liaison duties for the remainder of the war, which made him rather bitter.

In Bill's absence, George had taken over all of his oldest brother's business responsibilities. There was no alternative, since Arthur was already challenged in managing the accounting and staffing functions. The war added even more challenges to the survival of the business. The draft caused labor shortages and most supplies were sent to the troops. Price regulations were still in effect and the Owens were obliged to sell at low margins. The only hope for survival was to find more inventory. George was assigned this difficult and thankless task. Arthur had his own challenges, as the demand for store credit was high.

Upon his return from war, Bill resumed his role as managing director, but he began to participate less and less in the running of the company. George was forced to make important daily decisions without having the authority to do so. Meanwhile, the arguments between the two younger brothers became more serious. George spent his days devising ways to increase revenue and Arthur continually tried to block them. Without Bill's engagement, the conflict grew and a rift developed between George and Arthur that would never be bridged.

Bill's setbacks in the military had drained him of his desire to lead. The way to avoid having power removed was never to acquire it in the first place. As a result, his interest in the business was minimal, and his vision for the future nonexistent. Yet he never officially passed on the power of his position to either of his brothers. Thus the company was left without a strong leader. There was no one to create a shared vision to help unify the warring brothers.

Often Arthur would voice his complaints to his wife. At the same time, George was taking the problems home to his family. Naturally, this created a significant amount of tension within the extended family. As a result, gatherings became less frequent and the already strained lines of communication were almost severed.

The business itself was going through its hardest time since the Depression. With large numbers of men returning from war, new businesses were springing up and competition was growing. However, with rationing and price controls still in effect, it was becoming even more difficult to make a profit. Had it not been for an inquisitive customer, the business might very well have failed then. This customer approached Bill one afternoon in 1948 and asked to set up a payment plan. Richard Owens Pty. Ltd. became one of the first companies in the area to launch an installment purchase program. This service proved to be extremely lucrative and was responsible for a dramatic increase in profits.

More sophisticated financing options, however, complicated Arthur's credit activities. His stress culminated in a stroke in 1949. Arthur eventually returned to his duties, but the trauma was not without its consequences. His attitude deteriorated further, as did his ability to handle the day-to-day pressures of the business.

The self-service revolution

A new era in the grocery industry began in the 1950s with the rise of self-service supermarkets. George realized that, unless the business changed with the times, it would become obsolete. He lobbied for a transition to the self-service model. Arthur objected. The debate continued for years. But George believed that this decision was critical and that it was his duty to do everything in his power to keep the business alive. In August 1956, the flagship store was converted into the Owens' first self-service grocery. Arthur was incensed. After the first year of operation, the results clearly supported George's decision and the family began to convert the remaining stores to the self-service concept. After much debate, the name "Savemores" was chosen, and soon it appeared in bright red letters above each store.

Between 1956 and 1962 George actively pursued the growth of the business, through expansion of the self-service idea and through acquisition. Every deal brought an argument with Arthur. The pace and daily frustration eventually became too great and, in 1961, George suffered a nervous breakdown.

The third generation

The problems caused by family personalities were exacerbated when, in 1953, Bill's son Alan entered the business. Alan's mental and emotional stability were questioned. He was tactless, and his skills only qualified him for menial tasks. Yet, not long after joining the business, he was promoted to the position of store manager. Because of Bill's ongoing difficulties, his two brothers did not

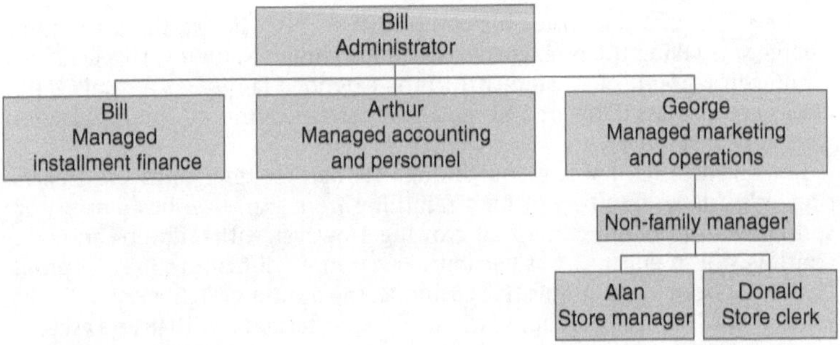

Figure E.2 Organization chart (1957)
Source: Derived from company information.

complain. They honored Bill's wishes to see his son appear successful. From his first day at the store, Alan proved to be a trial. At best he was unhelpful, and at worst he could be verbally disruptive. Still, he was allowed to continue. Bill's daughters chose not to be involved in the business.

Very early on in his children's development, George had decided that he did not want them involved in the family company. He felt that the grocery industry was too much work for too little reward. In addition, he did not want to subject his children to constant bickering. He wanted a happier and more prosperous life for his sons Richard and Donald and for his daughter Margaret. Richard, the oldest, graduated with a degree in pharmacy and returned home to open two independent pharmacies.

Richard's brother Donald was more drawn to the business and, in 1957, became the second cousin to join the company. (Refer to Figure E.2 for the 1957 organization chart.) George believed that any family member starting in the business should begin at the bottom and learn every detail of the organization through experience. Consequently, although it was clear that Donald was far more capable than Alan, he was given an entry-level job. Thus a precedent was set that all cousins would be compensated according to seniority.

After George's breakdown, Richard left his two pharmacies to join the family business and to help relieve his father's workload. After eighteen months, Richard had taken over most of his father's responsibilities and seemed to have a natural gift for the business. He realized that he preferred the challenge of the grocery industry to the stability of a pharmacy business. He found a manager for his own shops (which he later sold), so that he could focus all his energies on the family company.

Arthur had four children – John, Helen, Bruce and Judy. None appeared to be interested in becoming part of the family organization. But, eventually, feeling threatened by George's growing faction within the company, Arthur proposed that his own two sons join the business. (Refer to Figure E.3 for the 1963 organization chart.)

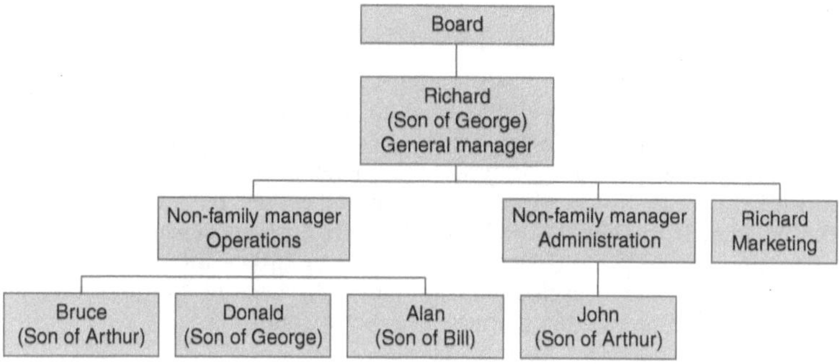

Figure E.3 Organization chart (1963)
Source: Derived from company information.

Although Bruce and John complied with their father's wishes, their participation was essentially in name only. Neither one showed any interest in learning about the organization, and both spent as much time as possible away from their work. For a while, this situation appeared to satisfy everyone. Arthur was placated, happy that his sons were involved and were there to support him, while Richard and Donald were free to run the operation without dissent. There was no animosity among the cousins, although they could not be described as close.

Over the years, however, Arthur pushed his sons further up in the organization. His primary concern was to try to ensure that they were always at the same level as Richard and Donald. Whenever one of his nephews received a promotion or a raise, he insisted that his sons be equally rewarded. As the pressure and responsibility on Arthur's sons increased, their uninterested attitudes became more of a problem. Non-family employees were particularly frustrated.

From 1961 to 1974 Richard led the company to unprecedented levels of growth. Following his father's and grandfather's entrepreneurial tradition, Richard opened liquor stores and expanded the business into the food service sector. These decisions would save the family business later on, during a time when grocery sales were slipping. He was appointed to the company's board in 1967.

In 1974 Arthur proposed that his son Bruce be appointed to the board. This was the last straw. Richard had devoted the previous thirteen years to the company, while Bruce had been much less involved. Richard had accepted the fact that others received lavish compensation for a fraction of the work because of the family practice of equal distribution of wealth. But he refused to jeopardize his authority and decision-making power by having someone with questionable ability and a problematic attitude on the board. This time the competition between his father and uncles had gone too far, and it had to stop.

Acknowledgments

This case study, IMD-3-1492 was written by Research Associate Colleen Lief and Professors John L. Ward and Joachim Schwass as a basis for class discussion rather than to illustrate either effective or ineffective handling of a business situation. The authors wish to thank Robin Neff, Monica Wagen and Alden Lank for their valuable contributions and express their appreciation to the IMD-Lombard Odier Darier Hentsch Family Business Research Center for its support of this project.

Appendix F
Case Study: Four Generations of the Owens Family (B)

IMD INTERNATIONAL

By late 1974, Richard had decided that he had no alternative. He had tried everything he knew to make peace in the business. Nothing had worked, so he delivered an ultimatum to the three other directors. They must either dissolve their active interests in the company, leaving Richard as managing director with a new board, or he would resign. Several company executives would likely go with him. An emergency board meeting was held in December, which Neville Dalby, the company accountant, attended. He tried to impress on those present the seriousness of the situation:

> If Richard resigns, in my opinion the action would eventually destroy the Owens empire. That means it would affect all shareholders, senior and junior. It also means that your credit would be destroyed.
>
> (Interview with Neville Dalby)

In January 1975, Richard handed the following note to his Uncle Bill:

> To the Directors, Richard Owens Pty. Ltd:
>
> I herewith tender my resignation from the company as from 21st January. This confirms the verbal notice given at the family meeting held late November last year at which I indicated that if nothing constructive was done to resolve the deadlock between family interests, then I would have to take this step. To date no action has been taken and I therefore have no alternative.
>
> Yours faithfully,
> Richard J. Owens

For over a month, members of the family tried to convince Richard to withdraw his resignation. Various verbal promises were made, but Richard had heard it all before. He realized that, if he backed down now, all his leverage would be lost. This was not a threat that could be issued twice. He decided to force a decision by presenting a list of demands:

1. The three senior Owens would retire from the company as of April 30, relinquish all duties, vacate their offices and cease to attend to the business in any form.
2. A new Board of Directors would be assigned as the governing party of the Operating Company.
3. Management responsibility and authority would be determined by position in the organization, not by position in the family.
4. Family members would cease to receive special privileges. Their contribution to the company would be evaluated by the same criteria used for non-family members.
5. All employees, including family members, would receive a salary in accordance with market value. Salaries were to be approved by the Operating Board.

At a March board meeting, the senior Owens brothers discussed Richard's letter. After intense debate, it was decided that the three would retire. The new arrangement only lasted a matter of months. Soon Richard realized that the meddling of the second generation would never end, even if they were not on the board. He decided in early 1976 that another solution was necessary.

Richard called a meeting with his brother and cousins to explore how to break up the company. It was decided that each branch of the family should freely select the part of the company it wanted to control. At that time Richard Owens Pty. Ltd. consisted of real estate, supermarkets, liquor stores and a warehousing operation.

Between June and November 1976, seven meetings were held to determine the feasibility of partitioning the company into three holdings equal in asset value, sales volume and operating profit. In addition, consideration was given to the following criteria: geography, risk and the desired lifestyle of each family. Seven months later, the 71-year-old family firm was officially divided among the branches of the family. The need for cooperative effort was gone; each family group was responsible for its own business. All were satisfied with what they had received.

After the break-up: Bill's and Arthur's holdings

Bill's family seemed to prefer a hands-off management style. It ended up maintaining ownership rights to the property, got out of the grocery business and later developed hotels. It hired non-family managers to handle the day-to-day operations. This proved to be a workable formula for Bill and his heirs.

Arthur's family fared worse. They continued to operate their stores for some time. However, involvement in multi-family real estate projects quickly led to the demise of Arthur's part of the business, which was closed in 1986.

After the break-up: George's holding

After the split in 1977, George adopted a more structured approach and formed a holding company comprised of liquor stores, supermarkets and real estate properties. The new shareholders were George and his wife (25 percent) and their three children, Margaret, Donald and Richard (25 percent each).

In the same year, to enable each member of the third generation to pursue his or her own interests and to avoid the conflicts that had affected the previous generation, George's holdings were divided again among his three children. George sold the liquor stores to Donald and the grocery stores to Richard. Margaret, who was already married and a mother, could participate in the real estate company and received dividends from its activities.

Donald built up his liquor store business to ten autonomously managed stores. Meanwhile Richard bought a store called Food Barn, which became a very successful discount supermarket chain.

Richard built a thriving retail business. But, when he could no longer finance growth internally, his banker insisted that he take the company public or sell it to a larger firm. Richard decided to sell the company to Australia's largest retailer in 1988. He worked for the new owner for a while but, feeling out of place in such a large company, he resigned.

Soon after selling his company, Richard formed RO Investments (Richard Owens Investments Company). (Refer to Figure F.1 for the evolution of the company since 1977.) According to Richard,

> We sold the supermarket business for cash. That's important because you then have to do something with it. It wasn't enough to have some shares and then merely play golf for the rest of our lives while those shares rose on the stock market. So we created a small investment company called RO-Investments, which was comprised of – in addition to myself – two key people.
>
> At the beginning, we were fortunate because we had cash on deposit and interest rates were high. But the recession hit Australia much sooner than the rest of the world. We had to do something else with our investment; we couldn't just leave it in the bank.
>
> I subsequently learned a lot, while on a sabbatical year at IMD, about how to write a family business mission statement and put to paper a family philosophy. However, I still did not have a clear vision of what was going to happen next.
>
> (Interview with Richard Owens)

Richard's son, David joined him in the business in 1992, after gaining experience in the financial services sector and after receiving an MBA from IMD. Father and son sat down together and looked at how David could fit into

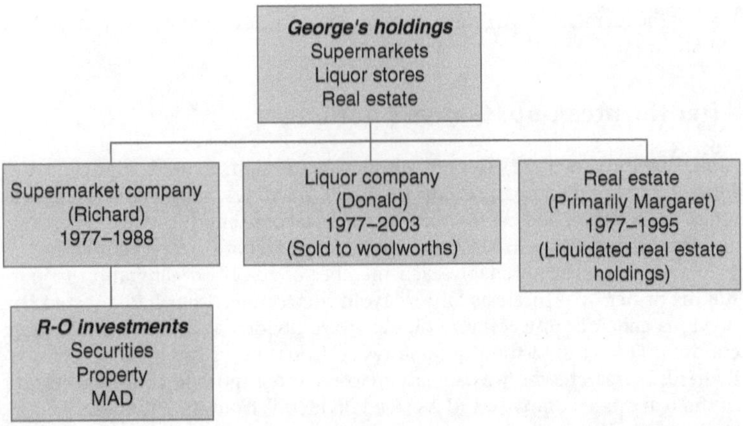

Figure F.1 The evolution of George's holdings
Source: Derived from company information.

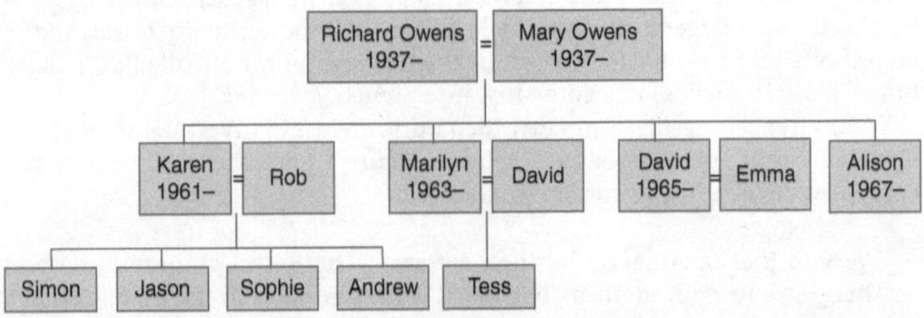

Figure F.2 Richard Owens's family tree (1995)
Source: Derived from company information.

RO-Investments in a way that would be beneficial for both him and for the company.

At first they concluded that it would be best for David to devote five years to working somewhere else. But spending three to five years in a large company would probably mean he would obtain more narrow functional experience rather than the generalist background he would need. Directly entering the family business seemed to be a better choice.

RO-Investments had begun looking for ways to expand by pursuing new business investments. Since the new businesses needed senior staff, a number of opportunities were available. So discussions were held with Richard's three daughters, Karen, Marilyn and Alison, to find out if they also wished to join the family business. (Refer to Figure F.2 for the Richard Owens family tree as of 1995.)

Enter the fourth generation

As Karen had expressed her preference to remain a full-time mother, Richard offered Marilyn, Alison and David jobs in specific areas of the family company. They had gained experience at American Express, Unilever and Citicorp, respectively. The three children agreed to join the company if they could work in Sydney, far away from headquarters. So, in 1993, they set up the Sydney office; it was called MAD (an acronym for Marilyn, Alison and David). Ownership of RO-Investments was divided into six equal parts among Richard, Mary and their four children. (Refer to Figure F.3 for the organization chart of RO-Investments.) The overall management of RO-Investments remained, however, in Richard's hands. He was the managing director and the chairman of the board and he held all of the voting shares.

Thanks to the geographical separation, the three members of MAD enjoyed a great deal of independence. But David was concerned that this autonomy could also result in a rift between family and non-family managers, even though profits from the business were reinvested in the company. No dividends were distributed to family. The only cash flow to the members of the fourth generation was as a result of being employed in the company. Family members were remunerated according to market conditions and no other special benefits existed.

Also in 1993, the members of the family took a holiday together and launched the first ever "family council" meeting. This was an opportunity for family members to express their wishes for the future. By the end of the meeting, everyone believed that the conflicts of the previous generation were not likely to be repeated with them.

Other family council meetings followed, and they included Richard's in-laws: Karen's husband Rob, who owned a surveying practice; Marilyn's

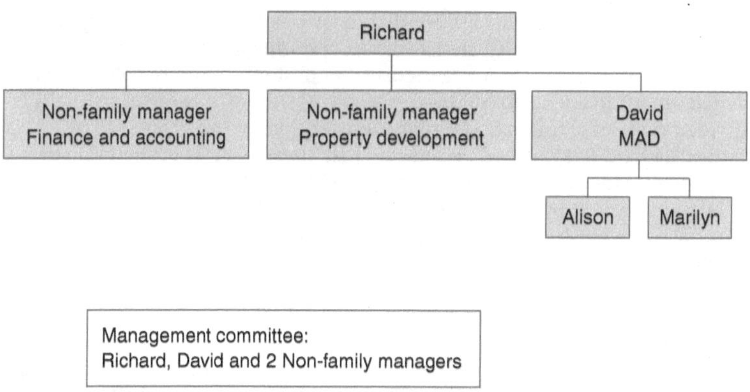

Figure F.3 RO-Investments Company
Source: Derived from company information.

husband David, who owned a property development firm (itself a family business); and David's wife Emma, a stay-at-home mother. They focused on sharing information about the company and its performance and on learning about family business principles and family constitutions. David commented:

> The meetings, however, were largely unsuccessful because we were not sufficiently aware of the serious nature of the business issues. The rules of the council were often broken and the succession issue was only briefly discussed. It will take some time to get a more mature approach to the way we handle these meetings, but we have made a good start.
>
> (Interview with David Owens)

By 1995 the succession process was still not formalized, even though there was a natural predisposition to assume that David – the only son – would take over. For his part, David was still concerned about the future:

> I am not sure that I want to be responsible for my siblings' wealth and risk the kind of traumas that happened in previous generations. I would like to be involved with a company that manufactures or processes products, but unfortunately I do not have enough financial power to impose my entrepreneurial dream. I think that the company should not be merely an investment company that acts as a store of wealth for the family, but rather it should be a company that produces something. It would provide a higher return, and I could create something that I could become involved in and gain pleasure from. That's the kind of business you can have fun with. Just sitting and watching shares grow doesn't really interest me.
>
> (Interview with David Owens)

Richard's reply

Being an entrepreneur, Richard wanted to keep control over his company for as long as possible. Ideally, he wished to continue as managing director for five years, then gradually to relinquish his position while remaining active as chairman. In Richard's opinion, the ownership of a company should be divided only after the management succession issue has been resolved. As a father, Richard felt satisfied because he had already accomplished one of his aims: to provide all his children with a good future.

His concern, though, was to find an appropriate structure for the succession of ownership and management of his company. Should they keep RO-Investments in its present form – a portfolio that could easily be divided among his heirs? Or should he reinvest in an operating business and take the potential risk of creating the same kinds of conflicts his uncles had experienced?

Richard could see that both David and Alison appeared to be suitable candidates for the position of CEO, but he felt reluctant to choose between them. He believed that showing favoritism broke all the rules of family behavior. He did not know how to proceed and what selection criteria he should use.

Richard was also concerned about the ownership of the company and about ways to solve the potential conflict of interest among heirs who were active in the business and heirs who were not. Passive members were more likely to give higher priority to dividends. Active members might have the tendency to plow profits back into the business, to make it stronger for the future.

To avoid these and other potential problems, Richard wondered if he should depart from the principle of dividing the business among his children equally. To ensure that company ownership went into the right hands, it might be necessary to treat the heirs differently. Richard had to wrestle with how to resolve his two roles: father and owner–manager.

Richard realized that the firm was at a major crossroads and that he needed to give serious thought to these issues. David suggested using an upcoming family council meeting to discuss the next steps concerning the family and its enterprise.

Acknowledgments

This case study, IMD-3-1493, was written by Research Associate Colleen Lief and Professors John L. Ward and Joachim Schwass as a basis for class discussion rather than to illustrate either effective or ineffective handling of a business situation. The authors wish to thank Robin Neff, Monica Wagen and Alden Lank for their valuable contributions and express their appreciation to the IMD-Lombard Odier Darier Hentsch Family Business Research Center for its support of this project.

Appendix G
Case Study: Four Generations of the Owens Family (C)

IMD
INTERNATIONAL

By 1995, all four of Richard and Mary's children had found their way back to Australia from adventures abroad and had become involved, to greater or lesser degrees, in the family company. As Richard yearned for a little more flexibility and free time, and was ever mindful of what happened when relatives failed to take an active role in their own futures, it seemed time to adopt a more formal approach to leadership at the Richard Owens Investments Company.

The decision to select David as the heir-apparent leader of the family firm was made swiftly by the four siblings. One by one, the sisters had decided to devote time to raising families and gradually withdrew from active day-to-day participation in operations. Since David returned to Australia with his MBA, his capabilities and business acumen had become increasingly obvious. While Richard remained at the helm of the enterprise, David was being groomed to take the reins one day.

Attendance at a family business course planted the seed in Richard's mind that a family constitution would be critical in preventing the trouble that had plagued the Owens family in the past from visiting the next generation. Richard was driven to secure the family's wealth and business for his children and grandchildren. He believed that a document as critical and complex as a family constitution did not suddenly materialize ready-made from a consultant's office. Rather it would emerge over time, from hard work and real communication. He felt strongly that no lawyer or accountant could do the required legwork. The Owens had to devote time, energy and caring to develop a solution that was the right fit for their philosophy and history. Richard firmly believed that, if the Owens clan was to have any chance of success, an open, inclusive, well-considered process must precede any written document. He said:

> My advice to other families is: Get the right structure and then continue to work at it. It sounds clichéd, but a family constitution is a living document.
>
> (Interview with Richard Owens)

Richard Owens Investments Company (RO-Investments) continued to administer the significant portfolio of stocks and bonds that represented the proceeds of the 1988 sale of Richard's previous retail business. In addition, the company owned, developed and managed commercial real estate projects, including small shopping centers, medium density housing and other commercial buildings.

As David grew into his leadership role, Richard began withdrawing from the day-to-day running of the business. He indulged his passion for wine and started a small vineyard and winery. This move gave both men a feel for what the future would hold and a deeper appreciation for each other's abilities. As Richard commented:

> I think that leaders of family businesses sometimes hold on too long. I say – move over and get into something else. Give your kids a chance at success.
>
> (Interview with Richard Owens)

Richard was the primary advocate for creating a mechanism, a blueprint for healthy family governance. But, over the three years from 1995 to 1998, the entire Owens family earnestly labored to craft a sound document to govern the family's relationship with the business. They worked consistently to develop the structure and institutions that could accomplish their goals. Through a patient, evolutionary process, the mechanisms for maintaining equality, freedom and communication among all branches of the family and business began to take shape. (Refer to Figure G.1 for a graphical representation of the Owens family constitution.)

The family's six shareholders (Richard, Mary and their four children) each held a trust; together, these owned the businesses through a Holding Trust. Each family trust appointed a representative to an owners' board, which in turn appointed the three members of the business board (Richard, David and the company's financial director).

The family's wishes and interests were brought to bear through the institution of a family council. All members of the Owens family were members of the council and could attend its two annual meetings, one of which included a family vacation. The expenses associated with the council's activities and with the family meetings were covered by company. The only officer of the family council was the chair, who was elected from among family ranks. Richard nominated Karen to be the first chair, in recognition of her seniority in the family and of her obvious interest in the business. Her nomination received unanimous approval from her siblings.

The chair of the family council was elected for a period of three years and acted as the conduit for communication between the family and the firm.

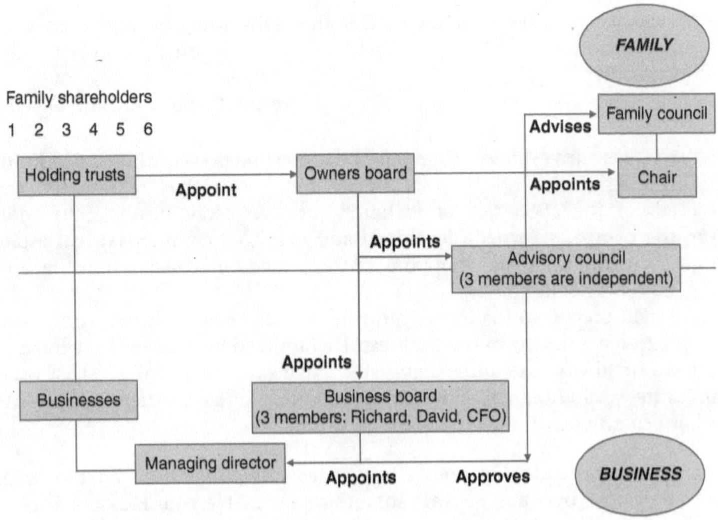

Figure G.1 Owens family constitution framework (1997–1998)
Source: Derived from company information.

The chair observed meetings of the advisory council, a body whose mission was to foment effective interaction between family and the business and to approve the selection of any new company managing director. At this time, the advisory council consisted of three outside directors who were appointed to three-year terms by the owners' board.

The Owens family constitution outlined the manner in which the various working bodies governed and served the interests of the family and of the business; it also set out specifics for position qualifications, meeting frequency, term limits and employment of family. Its basic tenets included provisions for dividend distribution, sale of shares, education of the next generation and entrepreneurial investment opportunities for family members.

By 1998, the preconditions for transition were complete. Richard had found a new business to care about; David had demonstrated the capacity to manage the enterprise; and the first family constitution – so important to preserving wealth and harmony – was adopted after five drafts and lots of discussion. It was clear that the constitution would be a work-in-progress for some time to come. But the Owens family was thrilled to have embarked on such a crucial journey and to have emerged on the other side – intact and with consensus. Taking this step toward sustainable governance gave it a real sense of accomplishment and stewardship.

This important period in the company's and family's history culminated in 1998, when David was appointed managing director of Richard Owens Investments Company, at the age of 33.

At various junctures, the four Owens children considered going their separate ways – financially. But in the end they always decided that the answer was "no." Richard believed that the real affection they shared, the expediency of higher returns possible as an investment block and lessons learned from the past led his children to stick together – in business and in life.

Acknowledgments

This is an abridged version of case study IMD-3-1494, available from www.ecch.ch. The case was written by Research Associate Colleen Lief and Professors John L. Ward and Joachim Schwass as a basis for class discussion rather than to illustrate either effective or ineffective handling of a business situation. The IMD-Lombard Odier Darier Hentsch Family Business Research Center provided support for this project.

Notes

The Cycle of Wealth

1. Lawless, Robert and Elizabeth Warren. "The Myth of the Disappearing Business Bankruptcy." *California Law Review*, Vol. 93, Issue 3, May 2005, 745–795. (Referenced by John Tozzi in *Business Week* article below.)
2. Tozzi, John. "As Bankruptcies Surge, Fewer Emerge." *Business Week.com*, June 23, 2009. http://www.businessweek.com/print/smallbiz/content/jun2009/sb20090623_271086.htm

1 The Cycle of Entrepreneurship

1. Attributed to Alexis de Tocqueville. Giuliani, Rudolph W. *Leadership Through the Ages: A Collection of Favorite Quotations*. New York: Miramax Books, 2003.

2 Generation One – The Entrepreneur

1. Attributed to Calvin Coolidge upon his retirement as president of board of directors of New York Life Company, 1933. In Maury Klein (ed.) *The Change Makers*. New York: Henry Holt and Co LLC, 2003.
2. "You've Got to Find What You Love." Text of commencement address delivered by Steve Jobs, *Stanford Report*, June 14, 2005. http://news-service.stanford.edu/news/2005/june15/jobs-061505.html
3. Attributed to Louis C. Gawthrop. *Public Service and Democracy: Ethical Imperatives for the 21st Century*. New York: Chatham House, 1998. From Getha-Taylor, Heather and Norma M. Riccucci (eds.) "Managing the 'New Normalcy' with Values-Based Leadership: Lessons from Admiral James Loy." *Public Administration Review*, Vol. 69, Issue 2 March/April 2009, 200–206.
4. Bottger, Preston. *Reinventing the Swiss Watch Industry: Management Lessons from Nicolas Hayek of Swatch*. IMD Tomorrow's Challenges, January 2010.
5. Mount, Ian. "Are Entrepreneurs Born or Made?" *CNN Money.com*, 9 December 2009. http://money.cnn.com/2009/12/09/smallbusiness/entrepreneurs_born_not_made.fsb/index.htm
6. Ferragamo, Salvatore. *Shoemaker of Dreams: The Autobiography of Salvatore Ferragamo*. Edinburgh: Chambers Harrap Publishers Ltd., 1957.
7. Zegna Group, Article by Joachim Schwass, IMD, 2000.
8. Silver, A. David. *The Entrepreneurial Life: How to Go for it and Get it*. New York: John Wiley & Sons, 1986.

9. Galbraith, John Kenneth. *The Age of Uncertainty*. Boston: Houghton Mifflin Co., 1977.
10. Frieden, Jeffry A. *Global Capitalism: Its Fall and Rise in the Twentieth Century*. New York: W.W. Norton & Co., 2006.
11. Drucker, Peter. *Managing in Turbulent Times*. New York: Harper & Row Publishers Inc., 1980.
12. Alcaly, Roger. *The New Economy*. New York: Farrar, Strauss and Giroux, 2003.
13. Drucker, Peter F. *The Essential Drucker*. New York: HarperCollins Publishers Inc., 2001.
14. Kotter, John P. *Matsushita Leadership: Lessons from the 20th Century's Most Remarkable Entrepreneur*. New York: Free Press, 1997.

3 Generation Two and Beyond – The Family Business

1. "A Family Portrait: Taking a Closer Look at Family-Run Companies." *Morgan Stanley Equity Research North America Strategy Report*, August 12, 2005.
2. "La Gamme Génération: Partager Notre Vocation d'Entrepreneurs." Oddo Asset Management Presentation in Geneva, September 23, 2009.
3. Coates, John C. and Reiner Kraakman. "CEO Tenure, Performance and Turnover in S&P 500 Companies." John M. Olin Center for Law, Economics, and Business Discussion, No. 595, 2007.
4. "CEO Turnover Remains High at World's Largest Companies." Booz Allen Hamilton, May 22, 2007.
5. Puig, Mariano, Sr. *FBN Newsletter*, 1999.
6. Sonnenfeld, Jeffrey. *The Hero's Farewell: When CEOs Retire*. New York: Oxford University Press, 1988.
7. Tagiuri, Renato and John Davis. "Bivalent Attributes of the Family Firm." *Family Business Review*, Vol. 9, Issue 2, 1996, 199–208.

5 The Future – The Family Office

1. From personal interview with Kathryn McCarthy.
2. From personal interview with Ben Oehler.
3. Leleux, Benoît, Joachim Schwass and Albert André Diversé. "Europe's Family Offices, Private Equity and Venture Capital." IMD and the European Private Equity & Venture Capital Association Special Paper, October 2007.
4. Burri, Myriam and Olivier Reymond. "The Family Office: Fleeting Trend or Lasting Values?" *Journal of Financial Transformation*, Issue 15, December 2005, 76–78.
5. Leleux, Benoît, Joachim Schwass and Albert André Diversé. "Europe's Family Offices, Private Equity and Venture Capital." IMD and the European Private Equity & Venture Capital Association Special Paper, October 2007.

6. Family Office Benchmark – Governance. "Results from the European Family Office Conference 2005." Campden Publishing Limited, 2005.
7. Curtis, Gregory. "Establishing a Family Office: A Few Basics." Greycourt White Paper No. 10, Greycourt & Co, September 3, 2001.
8. "Preserving Family Values: The Changing Role of the Family Office." Citing the Merrill Lynch/Campden Research European Single Family Office Survey, 2008 (from www.familiesinbusiness.net).
9. Ibid.
10. Ibid.
11. "Preserving Family Values: The Changing Role of the Family Office." *Families in Business Magazine* (online), No. 37, March/April 2008.
12. "Preserving Family Values: The Changing Role of the Family Office." Citing the Merrill Lynch/Campden Research European Single Family Office Survey, 2008 (from www.familiesinbusiness.net).

6 The Family Office: What to Keep Your Eye On

1. Aristotle. Nicomachean Ethics, Book X, Chapter 9.
2. Personal interview with Melissa Berman.
3. Wilkinson, Tara Loader. "Philanthropy as Enterprise." *Wall Street Journal Europe*, December 4–6, 2009, W12.
4. EVPA website, http://www.evpa.eu.com.
5. Wilkinson, Tara Loader. "Philanthropy as Enterprise." *Wall Street Journal Europe*, December 4–6, 2009, W12.
6. Wise Philanthropy Advisors website, www.wise.net.
7. New Philanthropy Capital website, http://philanthropycapital.org.
8. The name "Bonnier" is a French variant of the German first name "Gutkind."
9. Hudson, Kris and Rachel Emma Silverman. "Mall Heirs Battle Over Will – Melvin Simon Boosted His Wife's Inheritance, Sparking Challenge from His Daughter." *Wall Street Journal*, February 10, 2010, A-2.

7 Single-Family Office or Multi-Family Office?

1. Black, Pamela J. "The Rise of the Multi-family Office," www.financial-planning.com, April 27, 2010.
2. Johnson, Hilary (quoting Tom Livergood of Family Wealth Alliance). "Do You Need a Family Office?" *Barron's Penta* (online), September 28, 2009.

8 The Cycle of Entrepreneurship Continues

1. Burke, Edmund. *Reflections on the Revolution in France*. J. Dodsley, 1791.
2. De Visscher, François. "Bridging the Entrepreneurial Divide." *Families in Business*, Issue 27 July/August 2006.
3. Boldness in Business Awards. "Expert Opinions." *FT.com*, February 25, 2010.
4. "*Keeping the Business in the Family: A Study of Swiss Family Businesses.*" IMD and Lombard Odier, Lausanne, 2001.

9 How It All Comes Together – The Long-Term View

1. Rockefeller, John D., Jr. *Ten Principles: Address in Behalf of United Service Organizations*. New York, July 8, 1941.

Appendix D The Yale/Harvard Model of Endowment Investment: The Importance of Asset and Risk Management

1. Gold, Howard. "Tough Lessons for Harvard and Yale." *Real Clear Markets*, 17 August 2009, http://www.realclearmarkets.com.
2. Harvard Management Company Endowment Report: Message from the CEO, September 2009.
3. "Yale University Releases Endowment Figures." Yale University Office of Public Affairs, 22 September 2009, http://opa.yale.edu/news/article.aspx?id=6899.
4. Fabrikant, Geraldine. "Harvard and Yale Report Losses in Endowments." *New York Times*, 11 September 2009, www.nytimes.com/2009/09/11/business/11Harvard.html.

Index

GPSR Compliance
The European Union's (EU) General Product Safety Regulation (GPSR) is a set of rules that requires consumer products to be safe and our obligations to ensure this.

If you have any concerns about our products, you can contact us on

ProductSafety@springernature.com

In case Publisher is established outside the EU, the EU authorized representative is:

Springer Nature Customer Service Center GmbH
Europaplatz 3
69115 Heidelberg, Germany

www.ingramcontent.com/pod-product-compliance
Lightning Source LLC
LaVergne TN
LVHW090406210926
848480LV00002B/469
* 9 7 8 1 3 4 9 3 3 1 2 1 5 *